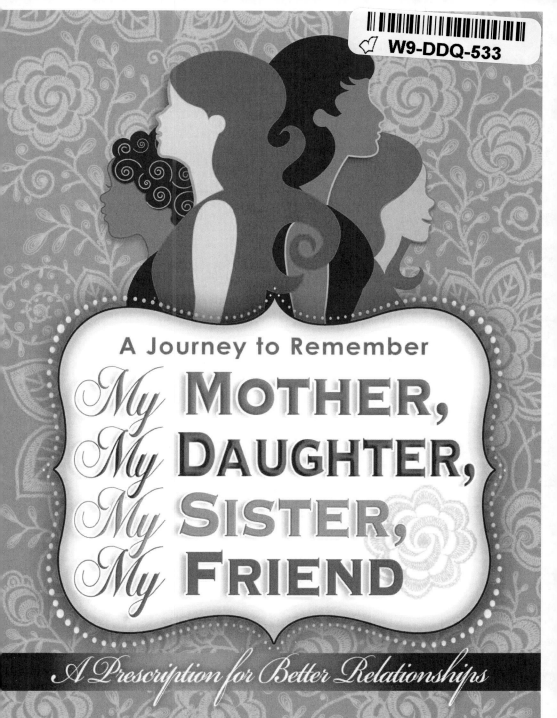

A Journey to Remember

*My* **MOTHER,**
*My* **DAUGHTER,**
*My* **SISTER,**
*My* **FRIEND**

*A Prescription for Better Relationships*

Chris Norris

# My Mother, My Daughter, My Sister, My Friend

## Chris Norris

**LOWBAR**
PUBLISHING COMPANY

905 South Douglas Avenue • Nashville, Tennessee 37204
Phone: 615-972-2842
E-mail: Lowbarpublishingcompany@gmail.com
Web site: www.Lowbarbookstore.com

Chris Norris, Author

Printed in the United States of America in 2013

© 2012 by Lowbar Publishing Company

ISBN: 978-0-9827151-8-5

Editor/Copy Editor: Honey B. Higgins
Layout Designer: Norah S. Branch
Graphic Art and Book Cover Designer: Norah S. Branch

For speaking engagements, workshops, and seminars, here is how you may contact the author:

Chris Norris: sisnorr@comcast.net or thehouseofnorris@gmail.com
Web site: www.thehouseofnorris.com

or

Lowbar Publishing Company
905 South Douglas Avenue
Nashville, TN 37204
Phone: (615) 972-2842
E-mail: Lowbarpublishingcompany@gmail.com
Web site: www.lowbarbookstore.com

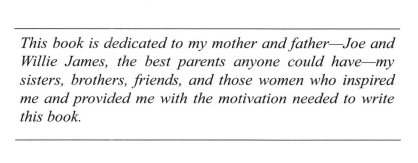

*This book is dedicated to my mother and father—Joe and Willie James, the best parents anyone could have—my sisters, brothers, friends, and those women who inspired me and provided me with the motivation needed to write this book.*

# Table of Contents

*"You can accept or reject the way you are treated by other people, but until you heal the wounds of your past, you will continue to bleed. You can bandage the bleeding with food, with alcohol, with drugs, with work, with cigarettes, with sex, but, eventually, it will all ooze through and stain your life. You must find the strength to open the wounds, stick your hands inside, pull out the core of the pain that is holding you in your past, the memories, and make peace with them."*

—*Iyanla Vanzant*

# *Acknowledgments*

This book is written in memory of my mother and father, Joe and Willie, who taught me what is most important in life. "Love the Lord your God with all your heart and with all your soul and with all your mind and with all your strength" (Mark 12:30). "If you have the faith as small as a mustard seed, you will say to this mountain, 'Move from here to there,' and it will move. Nothing will be impossible for you" (Matthew 17:20). I would also like to acknowledge my husband James, who gave me the time and space to write this book; my wonderful son, James III—a joy in my life; my beautiful and wise daughter, Lorraine; the precious jewels of my life—my grandchildren: Jamar, Kendall, Clarke, and Ezra; my sisters and brothers, friends, the students with whom I worked over the years (the reason for my writing the book), and the people I have met over the years who have inspired me more than anyone could ever know.

# *Introduction*

*"There is in every true woman's heart
a spark of heavenly fire, which lies dormant
in the broad daylight of prosperity,
but which kindles up and beams
and blazes in the dark hour of adversity."*
~Washington Irving, *The Sketch Book*

Life is short: We are born, we grow up, we go to school, we work, we marry, we have children, and we raise our families. We nurture those whom we love—we give them the best that we have. We give them every inch of our hearts, every single piece of our souls. We want our children to have a good life…a better life than we had. We want them to do work they love to do, be self-sufficient, and be able to care for themselves and have their own families (if they so choose). But after all that is done, then what? When the children have left the nest, we women retire—and these are the questions we ask ourselves: *Did I do all that I could have done? Could I have done more? Are my children happy? Did I give them the tools that they need in order to live their best lives? Do they know how much I love them?* We become reflective creatures as we think back on our lives, wishing we could have done some things better, yet honoring the special moments and cherishing the love.

After much discussion with my sisters and my friends on their relationships with others—and considering the information we have today—we could have all done a better job of communicating with our mothers, our sisters, and our daughters (and sons as well). As mothers, daughters, sisters, and friends, we all have complex relationships that require work, forethought, kindness, diligence, and patience. We are not perfect human beings.

This book—*My Mother, My Daughter, My Sister, My Friend*—is a look at the relationships we women develop with one another and the effects they have on our self-esteem, our personalities, and our careers—and how we see each other and the world in which we live.

It goes without saying that a woman's sister should be the person to whom she can turn at any time of the day or night. Her sister knows her better than anyone else and would make any sacrifice on her behalf. That is the myth and, thus, the reason why women feel so sad if their real sister relationship does not match up with the idealized one. It is the same with the mother-daughter relationship and, many times, the friend-friend relationship. They are not always easy.

As you are developing your identity while you mature, it is normal to compare yourself with your sister(s), mother, or friend(s) to see how you stack up—and who better to measure yourself against than the sister in the next room? Which one is smarter, which one is prettier, which one is more popular—which one does Mom and Dad admire most? Loving sister-sister relationships downplay that competitiveness…but sometimes the struggle to be seen as the best can lead to a lifetime of painful animosity.

Whether you have a great sister-sister or mother-daughter relationship that can be improved upon or not, you probably know that the initial mother-daughter bonding usually starts at an early age. When you are five, your mother is a goddess. You love dressing like your mom, putting on her makeup and jewelry, and, most of all, wearing her heels. You want to be just like your mom. At about the age of thirteen, you decide that you are smart enough that you no longer have to follow in your mother's footsteps. You want to make your own decisions, and listening to your mom is not what you want to do. You feel that she is completely out of touch with reality. However, somewhere between your twenties and your thirties, your mom may become your best friend again.

There is no relationship quite as precious and fulfilling as the one between a mother and her daughter, or a mother and her son. In an article (found on the Web site *DiscoveryHealth.com*) entitled "Our Mothers, Ourselves: Mother-Daughter Relationships," this is how one writer put it:

"It's the original relationship, and it's also a relationship that has been sentimentalized but not honored," says Lee Sharkey, Ph.D., who directs the Women's Studies program at the University of Maine at Farmington, where she teaches a popular course in mother-daughter relationships. "Women grow up and our energy is largely turned toward men, but the original love relationship is with a mother. If we as daughters don't acknowledge that, we're closing ourselves off from a great source of power and fulfillment and understanding of ourselves."

What this means is that a woman's mother-daughter relationship (with her mother) has a bearing on her sister-sister relationship, and then on her own role as a mother to her own daughter.

This book was written for sisters around the world—for mothers, daughters, grandmothers, aunts, cousins, and friends as well. In a manner of speaking, we are all sisters. Yes, we are all different—different races, different creeds, different nationalities, different sizes, with different statuses—but, we are sisters nonetheless.

It is my goal to share the reflections and understandings I have gained throughout my life regarding women's relationships. I am not a clinical psychologist or psychiatrist, but, rather, a mother, a daughter, a sister, and a friend. I was a school counselor and this also helped shape my ideas and opinions about relationships. As I examined my relationship with my mother and my three sisters, I began to consider birth order. Even though I have always felt comfortable with my sisters, my relationship was/is very different with each of them. In addition, I have read some very good books about this, which has helped me to understand my own family and friend relationships. (I have included these references in my resource list in the back of the book.) My observations and analysis are based on my personal experiences, and are my opinions alone (and are not meant to diagnose or treat any mental illnesses). This book is for information, education, and sometimes entertainment purposes only.

In this book, I will discuss the family order: *Were you the oldest child? The middle child? The baby?* It matters. I will also discuss how to embrace the differences between your siblings and your mother, and, ultimately, how to become a better mother, daughter, sister, and friend.

This is my journey. As you read this book, it will become your journey. Care to join me on this ride?

# Chapter One

# The Family Birth Order

*"In family life, love is the oil that eases friction,
the cement that binds closer together,
and the music that brings harmony."*
~Eva Burrows

Everyone has a birth order: you, your friends, your family members, your teachers, your co-workers—everyone. Your birth order is one of the most important aspects of your uniqueness. While other factors (such as age, race, and gender) all play a role in shaping one's personality, research indicates that *the number-one factor* which influences personality is birth order. One's *birth order* is referring to his/her rank in his/her family (i.e., firstborn, middle-born, last-born, only child, "only-born," or twin). We must not overlook the fact that age, race, gender, and family background are factors that are extremely important in shaping our personalities also.

A child's place in the birth order can have an effect on how he or she sees him- or herself. Research on birth order, sometimes referred to as *ordinal position*, shows that firstborn children (who often take the lead over the other children in the family) are more likely to go to college than children in any other position in the family. These statistics apply to "typical families" and cannot be the measuring stick for all families.

Having grown up with three sisters, I realized at a very early age that sisters are different from each other. I became aware of the conflicts that could occur between sisters. I was the third sister—therefore, there were many times when I felt caught in the middle. I was the "middle child." The middle child, according to some studies, seems to have the most negative outlook on his/her lot in life; however, I did not always feel that I fit the mold for the middle child (in that respect). For those typical middle children, a parent can help combat those feelings by pointing out to a middle child that, in a sense, he or she has the best of both worlds. After all, the middle child has both younger siblings and older siblings—and is both a big sister and a little sister. Younger children always want to be able to do the things older siblings are allowed to do; and older siblings may feel as though the younger siblings get away with things that they were not able to get away with when they were the same age.

In my childhood years, my older sisters often got away with telling me what to do and what not to do. In fact, my eldest sister constantly told me and my siblings what to do. She was "the boss"—the self-appointed boss. And I did not like that. But what I have learned is that the firstborn in a family is accustomed to being the center of attention, because at one point in time, he or she was the only child. This oldest sibling is generally very controlling, and may even respond to the birth of the second child by feeling unloved and neglected. The older sibling may either develop competent, responsible behavior, or become very discouraged in life. And sometimes, he or she will strive to protect and help others, and will strive to please— thus accomplishing goals beyond what the younger siblings accomplish.

In reflecting on my family dynamic over the years, I have noticed that it has been a trend for my oldest sister to always tell the other family members what to do. As I have previously stated, I did not like it and I do not think my other siblings cared for it, either. I think that the second-eldest sister experienced as much frustration as I did; however, she seemed to handle the situation better than I did. Perhaps she just knew how to disguise her feelings better than I did. I felt that she and my eldest sister were a bit more competitive with each other. I feel as though the second-eldest sister wanted her voice to be heard, just as I wanted my voice to be heard.

Meanwhile, the sister who is younger than I am (the youngest of all four sisters) appeared to have no voice at all. She did tend to harbor anger and resentment (passive-aggressive) and, as a young child, would fight from time to time. I know that was probably the only way she felt that she could be heard.

5

Based on my family's and my siblings' circumstances alone, it is evident that birth order is believed to have a lasting effect on a person's psychological development. If you stop and examine the way you and your family communicate today versus how you communicated years ago, you will realize that your means of communication with each other are still basically the same. Some researchers challenge the idea that birth order and psychological development are closely related, yet birth order continues to have a strong presence in psychology and popular culture today.

Alfred Adler was one of the first theorists to suggest that birth order influences personality. He expressed his view that birth order determines how we make friends, with whom we fall in love, and the jobs we choose. As we look at our own family structure, it is evident that the firstborn is not very happy when another child is born and receives more attention than he/she has received. Adler felt that birth order can leave an indelible impression on an individual's style of life—which is his or her way of dealing with the tasks of friendship, love, and work.

According to Adler, firstborns are "dethroned" when a second child comes along, and this may have a lasting effect on them. Younger and only children may be pampered and spoiled, which can also affect their later personalities. Additional birth-order factors that should be considered are the span of years between siblings, the total number of children, and the changing circumstances of the parents over time.

Since Adler's time, the influence of birth order on the development of personality has become a controversial issue in psychology. Among the general public, it is widely believed that personality is strongly influenced by birth order—but some psychologists dispute this. I, for one, consider it to be a very valid theory.

So when I grew up and became a school counselor, I began to look closely at the order of the family members. I believe it is a determining factor which influences how we relate to adults, our siblings, and others. I also believe that the behavior which one learned in his/her early years is the same behavior that he/she will continue to exhibit throughout life—unless he/she makes an effort to change that behavior.

I recently conducted a survey to glean some ideas about how differently women may feel about themselves and others, depending on their position in their families. They were asked how they compared to their sisters. The oldest in the family described herself as brilliant, loving, competent, the best, and proud. The younger sisters did not see the older sister as she saw herself; they described the older sister as controlling, bossy, and not always easy to talk to. The middle child saw herself as caring and patient, a good listener, and having the easiest time of all of them in making friends. The other members of the family described the middle child much the way she described herself.

The youngest child described herself as quiet, shy, and someone who struggled to meet the expectations of others; her sisters agreed with her. The youngest sister also felt as though she was unable to achieve all that she was capable of achieving because of the following:

- No one listened to her.
- Family members did not think that what she had to say was important.
- She was seldom able to show what she was capable of.
- She felt pushed aside.

She was also described as attentive, patient, a good listener, respectful, and true to herself, she loves her parents and loves family, and she is one who is encouraging, loving, and forgiving.

The following "typical" characteristics of birth order were adapted from Don Dinkmeyer, Gary D. McKay, and Don Dinkmeyer Jr., outlined in *Parent Education Leader's Manual*, Coral Springs, Florida, CMTI Press, 1978).

*Only Child (Only-born)*
- Child pampered and spoiled.
- Feels incompetent because adults are more capable.
- Is center of attention; often enjoys position. May feel special.
- Self-centered.
- Relies on service from others rather than own efforts.
- Feels unfairly treated when he or she doesn't get their way.
- May refuse to cooperate.
- Plays "divide and conquer" with parents to get their own way.

*First Child, First-born*
- Is only child for a period of time; used to being center of attention.
- Believes must gain and hold superiority over other children.
- Being right, controlling, and often important.
- May respond to birth of second child by feeling unloved and neglected.
- Strives to keep or regain parent's attention through conformity. If this fails, chooses to misbehave.
- May develop competent, responsible behavior or become very discouraged.
- Sometimes strives to protect and help others.
- Strives to please.

*Second Child*
- Never has parent's undivided attention.
- Always has sibling ahead who's more advanced.
- Acts as if in a race, trying to catch up or overtake first child.
- If first child is "good," second child may become "bad." Develops abilities first child doesn't exhibit. If first child successful, may feel uncertain of self and abilities.
- Might rebel.
- Often doesn't like position. Feels "squeezed" if third child is born.
- May push down other siblings.

*Middle Child of Three*
- Has neither rights of the oldest sibling, nor the privileges of the youngest.
- Feels life is unfair.
- Feels unloved, left out, "squeezed" out.
- Feels like he or she doesn't have a place in the family.
- Becomes discouraged and a "problem child" or elevates self by pushing down other siblings.
- Is adaptable.
- Learns to deal with both oldest and youngest sibling.

*Youngest Child*
- Behaves like only child.
- Feels everyone else is bigger and more capable.
- Expects others to do things, make decisions, and take responsibility.
- Feels the smallest and weakest. May not be taken seriously.
- Becomes the boss of the family in getting service and their own way.
- Develops feelings of inferiority or becomes "speedier" and overtakes older siblings.
- Remains "the Baby." Places others in service to him or her.
- If youngest of three, often, allies with oldest child against middle child.

The middle child of three usually behaves differently from the middle child of a large family. The middle children of large families are often less competitive—as parents do not have as much time to give to each child and so the children learn to cooperate in order to get what they want.

Only-born, only children usually want to be adults—so they do not relate to peers very well. When they become adults, they often believe that they have finally "made it" and can now relate better to adults as peers.

During their formative years, only-born, only children live primarily in the world of adults. They must learn how to operate in an adult world.

Do you recognize any of these characteristics in you?

As a middle child, I never wanted to cause problems for anyone and always wanted everyone to get along. I remained quiet then and I remain quiet now—even when I do not agree with negative statements that are made. I have always tried to stay away from confusion, and never wanted anyone to have hurt feelings over situations which were experienced or statements that were made to family members.

When talking to a friend of mine, who is also a middle child, she told me several stories about her older sister and how she had always been in competition with her, and the negative statements that were always directed at my friend by her sister. The competition that started years ago still exists today.

Competition between sisters is very common. This can be corrected (which I will explain more fully in chapter 9, "Empowering Women"). If you are a woman with a sister, then merely hearing the word *sister* will probably evoke a strong emotion in you. For some women, thinking about their sisters conjures up a warm, fuzzy feeling—a wonderful feeling of love and companionship. But for others, these thoughts can provoke anxiety and even anger. Women can and will be very vocal when it comes to their sisters. They do not usually remain neutral about their sisters (or their brothers, for that matter). For most women, the thought of sisters and sister relationships can bring back beautiful memories or can bring back memories that they would rather forget. We would like to have that idealized relationship that is imagined to be the most nurturing and satisfying bond possible. But this simply is not always the case.

With all of the differences that we have as sisters, I can tell you that the "sisterhood is better than any friendship" concept makes a whole lot of women feel inadequate and left out—when speaking about women without sisters; but also, women with sisters can find themselves in sister relationships that require a lot of work, love, and support. There are women who have nothing in common with their sisters—and women whose sister is their best friend. This concept seems to stem from our cultural ideal of the traditional family—*two married, healthy, heterosexual parents, and at least two healthy, attractive, and charming children, with two dogs*—which undermines the value of the primary, loving relationships that fall outside of that description. Not everyone will fit into that mold.

In our society, we have been made to feel that we can never be as happy and fulfilled as when we are a part of those "traditional families." But you and I both know that this is not true. Even though we may not come from perfect families or have perfect relationships with our *mothers, daughters, sisters,* or *friends*, we can make the most of these relationships by working to *understand who our loved ones are and helping them to understand who we are*.

In her new book, *You Were Always Mom's Favorite!: Sisters in Conversation throughout Their Lives*, linguist Deborah Tannen explores relationships between sisters and, as she told NPR's Susan Shemberg, "There is double meaning of the word bond...the bond of a connection and the bond of bondage." In an excerpt from the book, Tannen writes about discussing sisterhood with a group of women at a party. One woman said, "When we meet we can't get enough of each other. When we ride in a car together, we laugh about past experiences, repeat old jokes, and discuss things that only a family member would understand. We know what the other person is going to say before we say it. We decided to take vacations together." This discussion about sisterly bond and how much fun and enjoyment it is to have a sister prompted another woman to say, "I have always wished I had a sister."

Well, I *have* three sisters. I love them dearly, but for every time one of them has finished my sentence or laughed at an inside joke—based on a single word, phrase, or gesture—I can think of another time when one of them said things that were very painful, made fun of my ideas, made me sick with worry, reminded me of how imperfect I am, or disagreed with everything that I suggested.

I can think of another time when one of my sisters said something that really hurt my feelings. An example of that is whenever I am told "That's the way you are," or "That's the way you *all* are." In saying the latter, she was referring to the behavior of other members of the family. That statement, when said to anyone, can be a painful put-down. One's saying that to or about you seems to suggest that something is wrong with you—when the fact is that all of us are the way we are and all of us are different. Thus, that statement does not have to have a negative connotation.

I was not surprised to read the rest of Tannen's story, in which the woman admitted to the author privately that she and her sister had not spoken to each other for a year, following an enormous falling out over money. Now that is what I call "being *real*"!

In the book *Sibling Relationships: Their Nature and Significance across the Lifespan*, editors Michael E. Lamb and Brian Sutton-Smith help to convey the point that sibling relationships—good or bad—last an entire lifetime. They point out that the lifespan view proposes that development is continuous, and that all relationships change over time, and that any effects of birth order may be eliminated, reinforced, or altered by later experiences.

As I reflect on my own life, I know that I would have made many different decisions, had I had more information about the sibling order. Keep in mind, as you read this book, to think about all members of your family—but continue to focus on your sisters and female relationships. Take a look at the past and the relationship you had with your family and think about the things you would change…and remember that it is never too late to change. You can mend relationships, you can heal any hurts you may have caused one of your siblings, and you can start over, no matter what your age is.

Think about the conflicts you had and how those problems were handled. Look at how your life was and think about how you want your life to be now. *How can you change the dynamics of those family and friend relationships?* The important thing to remember here is that you cannot change anyone else—you can only change *you*. So, ask yourself these questions: *What do I want for myself, my daughter, my sister, my friend—and how am I going to make it happen? How am I going to use my birth order to improve the characteristics that I have developed? How am I going to be a* better mother, daughter, sister, *and* friend?

As far as eliminating problems that stem from the birth order, parents can help by attempting to encourage each child to see him- or herself as a unique individual—thus avoiding comparing him or her with his or her siblings or others. Of course, this does not happen in every household… especially in today's world, where parents are extremely busy and generally both parents work; in this case, *all* of the children can easily get lost in the shuffle of life.

You can use the knowledge of birth order to find out how to get along better with family, co-workers, and—for the purpose of this book—*your mother, daughter, sister,* and *friend.*

In chapter 2, I pose this question: *How do you stack up?* We now know that our birth order has an effect on our lives, our careers, and our relationships. Are you satisfied with your relationships as they are? Are there changes that you would like to make to them? If so, what are those changes? It is worth taking a few extra moments to further address the traits resulting from the birth order—and both the following blog and chapter 2 touch on this. As you read chapter 2, you will be able to examine yourself and your family members as well.

---

*I am the second child of 11. My eldest sister who is 2 years older than me fits the firstborn mold perfectly. I always chose to be different than my sister. As a child, if she liked pink or red, I liked blue. She loved chocolate, so I chose butterscotch or vanilla. She loved rock music as a teen in the early 60s and I chose classical or folk music—and so on. She spent her money as fast as she earned it and I saved. I do remember doing some of those things deliberately just to be different.*

*My children were born 5 years apart and the firstborn was a boy and the second a girl. They were both high achievers, albeit very different in personalities. They were both like firstborns because of the age difference and sex difference.*

*~Anonymous Online Blogger*

---

# Chapter Two

# How Do You Stack Up?

*"Families are like fudge—mostly sweet with a few nuts."*
~Author Unknown

As a middle child, yes, I often felt caught in the middle. As I stated earlier, whenever there were disagreements, I tried to stay out of the confusion. As a young child growing up, I was quiet and did not talk a lot when I was told "what to do" and "what not to do" by my sisters. As an older teenager, I was more outspoken and wanted to be heard. *Can anyone hear me?* seemed to be my mantra. Like most teenagers, I felt that I was capable of making my own decisions. There was a bit of a defiant streak to my nature—an independent streak which relayed that *I am my own person.*

While I was striving to be heard, I was concerned that two of my sisters were not as vocal about things as I was (when they should have been). No doubt, birth order had a lot to do with that reality.

As you can see, the dynamics created by birth order are always present. Some people might think, *Why should I care about birth order? What difference does it make?* Well, birth order is really the science of understanding your place in the family line, which affects the way you relate to people in your world. It affects the way you relate to your co-workers and your friends. Were you born first? Second? Third? Or, even farther down that line? And how do you stack up against your siblings?

### Which Trait Fits You Best?

---

*"We all grow up with the weight of history on us.
Our ancestors dwell in the attics of our brains
as they do in the spiraling chains of knowledge
hidden in every cell of our bodies."*
~Shirley Abbott

---

I know that it will be women who will mostly read this book, because we women care about our sisters, mothers, daughters, and friends. Yes, men do also, but they do not necessarily like to sit and analyze relationships the way women do. It is just a matter of fact. There is nothing wrong with it. We women are just the way we are, and I, for one, like it…*most of the time.*

At this moment, you are probably thinking back on your childhood and remembering incidents with your siblings: fights, collaborations, moments of secrecy, and so forth. These can be wonderful memories, or they can be thorns in your side. One thing you can be sure of is this: your personality is the same now as it was years ago (when you were a child). Sure, perhaps you have learned to control your temper. Perhaps you have learned good manners and know how to be charming—but basically, your personality is the same.

Which of the following personality traits describes you the best? (You will not meet all the criteria in a certain list of traits. Just choose the list that has the most items that seem to describe you.)

A. ***Perfectionist:*** dependable; conscientious; loyal; well-organized; trustworthy; a leader; a critical thinker; serious; needs to have all the information before making a decision.

B. *Mediator:* compromising; political; does not like conflict; tactful; loyal to peers; has many friends; a nonconformist; reserved; used to not having attention.

C. *Manipulative:* polite; blames others; loves attention; is persistent; is a people person; a natural salesperson; talented; warm and loving; and loves surprises.

D. *Little adult at an early age:* very thorough; calculating; high achiever; self-motivated; careful; avid reader; black-and-white thinker; talks in extremes; does not like failure; has very high expectations for self; enjoys interacting with people who are older or younger.

You might notice that this test seemed easy because the first 3 points—A, B, and C—listed traits according to the birth order: the oldest to the youngest in the family.

If you can relate more to "A," then it is a very good bet that you are a firstborn in your family. If you can relate to B, then chances are you are a middle-born (second-born of three children, or, possibly, third-born of four).

But what about the traits of D? It describes the only child. In the past few years, more and more families are having fewer children—and there are many "only" children who have no siblings. When looking at the only child versus the firstborn, one way they are different is that the only child is an extreme version of a firstborn. "Only" children have many of the same characteristics of firstborns, but in many ways they are in a class all by themselves.

### Firstborns Are Leaders

Statistics show that firstborns often fill positions of high authority or achievement (such as *Who's Who in America?*). And many of them are Rhodes scholars and university professors.

Presidents and church pastors are often firstborns, too. Twenty-eight out of forty-four U.S. presidents (64 percent) have been firstborn children, or functioned as (played the role of) firstborns. (This is when a child whose next closest same-sex sibling is five or more years older than him or her.) Eight of the eleven people who ran for president in the 2008 election were firstborn sons—or a firstborn daughter—in their families.

A number of our presidents were born later in their families. Some were born last—but in all cases they were the firstborn males in the family. That tells me that they had excellent chances of developing firstborn traits and functioning as firstborns. Being the first in the family or the firstborn male in the family helped those candidates to develop leadership skills which would be needed to serve as president.

Of course, some U.S. presidents have been middle children and a few have been last-born. Ronald Reagan was a last-born—the baby of the family.

In the 2008 U.S. presidential election, each of the final four contenders for the biggest job in the world was an only child; Barack Obama functioned as an only child, since his half-sister was nine years removed from him. There was also a firstborn daughter: Hillary Clinton—and two firstborn sons: Mike Huckabee and John McCain. There is definitely something unique about firstborns. They are true leaders.

### *Hollywood*

In Hollywood, you will find that many stars who were later-born children are comedians. Babies of the family who are loved by millions of movie and television fans include Eddie Murphy, Ellen DeGeneres, Whoopi Goldberg, Jay Leno, Steve Carell, Billy Crystal, Danny Devito, Drew Carey, and Jim Carrey.

It should be noted, however, that not all comedians are last-born. Bill Cosby, one of the greatest comedians of all time, is a firstborn. He also holds a doctorate degree and is a perfectionist. He gave all of his children names beginning with "E" to remind them to always seek excellence.

Other firstborn entertainers and actors include Matthew Perry, Jennifer Aniston, Angelina Jolie, Brad Pitt, Chuck Norris, Reese Witherspoon, and Ben Affleck.

Only-born children who are well known for their dramatic and sometimes comedic roles include Robert DeNiro, Laurence Fishburne, Anthony Hopkins, James Earl Jones, Tommy Lee Jones, William Shatner, and Robin Williams.

Newscasters and talk-show hosts on television are often firstborns and the only-born children. One of the more well-known, firstborn talk-show personalities is Oprah Winfrey, of course, who was also nominated for an Academy Award in her first movie, *The Color Purple.* She is a true example of a firstborn who was born to excel in everything she does in life.

### *Your Personality*

Newspapers and morning news shows have debated the issue that latter-born children may choose careers that include risky behavior; however, twenty-one of the first twenty-three astronauts who traveled into space were firstborns.

One's going off that data alone may cause him/her to question the above statement as factual. When scientists looked at the data, they found that the evidence just did not hold up. Two studies from the past three years finally found measurable effects: one's position in his/her family does indeed affect both his/her IQ and personality. Considering this, it may be time to reconsider birth order as a real determining factor of who and what we grow up to be.

---

*"If you don't believe in ghosts,*
*you've never been to a family reunion."*
~Ashleigh Brilliant

---

Decades of research indicated that birth-order was not a true science. It can be difficult to explain because family size can create differences as well as similarities in family members. Birth order is linked to family size; however, a child from a two-kid family will have a different psychological development than a child from a family of five.

There are many reasons why family size could affect our behavior and personalities. A couple's having more children means that parental resources (money, time, and attention) have to be spread more thinly. The family size is associated with many important social factors, such as education and wealth. For example, wealthier, better-educated parents typically have fewer children and are able to provide more educational opportunities for the children. If astronauts are more likely to have well-educated, comfortable parents, then they are also more likely to come from a smaller family and thus are more likely to be firstborns.

Whether birth order affects intelligence has been debated inconclusively since the late 1800s, although the sheer size of the study

(about 250,000 Norwegian conscripts) and the rigorous controls for family size make this study convincing.

Some scientists believe that birth order influences whom we choose as friends and spouses. Firstborns are more likely to associate with firstborns, middle-born with middle-born, last-born with last-born, and only children with only children. The adage that "opposites attract" is not always true. We find that people tend to resemble their spouses in terms of personality. If spouses have similar personality traits, and personality correlates with birth order, then spouses should correlate on birth order.

The evidence seems to be shifting back in favor of our common beliefs that our position in the family does affect who we become, who we marry, and whom we choose as friends. A Norwegian study shows a slight effect on intelligence. The relationship study shows that oldest, middle, youngest, and only children differ in some way—yet it gives no indication as to how.

Still, people will always try to make sense of the world through the prism of birth order—and as a woman, I believe it is an interesting way to analyze our relationships and lives.

### A Look at Yourself

Were you the bossy older sister, the middle child, or the spoiled baby of the family? As a kid, a big part of your identity is wrapped up in your place in the family, and some psychologists believe that the traits which you exhibit as a child will be the same traits that you will exhibit as an adult. These characteristics do not go away—even when you are no longer fighting with your little brother over the TV remote, or with your older sister over what TV program to watch. According to some researchers, your ending up as a CEO or a street bum might be more the result of an accident of birth than anything else. *So how do you stack up?* If you like what you see, then bravo; but if you do not like what you see, then change it. It is never too late to change. Reinvent yourself. Try something new.

As I discussed previously, early twentieth-century psychiatrist Alfred Adler was the first to propose a psychological theory of birth order. He believed that firstborns were loved and supported unconditionally until a younger sibling came along—at which point the eldest was "dethroned."

As a result, he theorized, the oldest child in a family is most likely to suffer from anxiety and depression, and turn to substance abuse in order to deal with excessive responsibilities (e.g., taking care of younger siblings), and the loss of a once-exalted position. The youngest child, Adler wrote, would be pampered and overindulged, leading to self-centeredness and a lack of empathy. In Adler's theory, middle children were most likely to be successful. However, this is not what other psychologists believed. (It might be worthwhile to note that Adler himself was a middle child.)

Throughout most of the twentieth century, Adler's theories of birth order were considered slightly controversial. Most people seem to believe that one's personality is affected by his or her place in the family, and stereotypes about these supposed character traits abound—i.e., the overachieving perfectionist must be the oldest, the show-off performer the youngest—but there was actually no real evidence to concretely link personality traits specifically to birth order, as opposed to other contributing factors. Others feel that there is a correlation between family size, education, and wealth. Factors such as high expectations, good schools, and social influence may carry as much weight in the observation that presidents and astronauts have been predominately firstborns (another factor).

Several recent studies, however, show scientific correlation between birth order and specific attributes. A huge Norwegian study involving nearly 250,000 people found that eldest children scored slightly higher on IQ tests than younger siblings. One theory is that the oldest child, by definition, had a greater share of his/her parents' attention as a baby, and over time will have more cumulative adult attention than his younger siblings; this correlates positively with reasoning and vocabulary skills.

There are plenty of factors that play into our understanding of birth order and how we are affected by birth order; but there are so many variables that change the dynamics of the family. One variable is, of course, families consisting of an only child—but then there are large blended families (where there might be two, three, or more middle children), blended families, older-child adoptions, and siblings with greater-than-average age differences. As our definition of "family" expands—with many non-traditional family groupings affecting what might be a child's traditional place in the family—the study of birth order and its impact on personality will also need to broaden its own definitions in order to keep up.

One study in the U.K. found that the majority of mothers believed that their youngest child would have the happiest life, while they thought the eldest was more likely to succeed academically, but also to struggle with anxiety and depression. *Are these beliefs passed on to their children, thus becoming a self-fulfilling prophecy?*

Whether you are the first, middle, youngest, or only, your personality and behavior are likely to be shaped by your birth order in the family. Your parents may have unwittingly perpetuated the stereotypes, depending on their own sibling relationships and their beliefs in whether birth order matters.

My brother, the oldest member of the family, was always considered to be "very smart" and we (the family as a whole) always listened to his stories. After all, he was very smart, right? And we held on to every word he uttered. I believe we thought that if we listened hard enough, we could become as smart as he was.

When my brother went away to college, I (along with my other siblings) wanted to measure up to his standards. I considered him a role model and wanted to follow in his footsteps. He was someone whom people listened to and also looked up to as a role model.

I am not sure what my oldest brother's IQ was, but I do feel that he could/can communicate with anyone and everyone, and can make anyone feel at ease. I have never seen anyone who does not enjoy talking to him—and, believe me, he always has something to say. (Better yet, what he has to say is always *interesting*.) Of course, that takes more than intelligence. It takes real charisma.

My oldest brother is a born leader and is very successful academically. He is comfortable in his own skin. This is a trait of the oldest-born. He has also motivated his own children to be successful. As for my youngest brother—the baby—well, he has been very successful as well. He is happy as well, but he still loves to be pampered and adored because he is…well… the *baby*. That tends to be a common trait among those who are the youngest child in a family. They show love toward others, and love attention and pampering. We can see that birth order can be a factor in deterring your success, but it certainly is not an exact science.

It has been said that a parent may also subconsciously identify with the child who holds the spot in the family they themselves filled. A baby-of-the-family mom might have a very different attitude than does a middle-child mom toward their youngest child's spotlight-stealing adventures. In the U.K. study, a higher percentage of mothers admitted to identifying most with their eldest child.

It must be noted that once you are an adult, changes can be made. The science may indicate that you have some personality traits and tendencies based on your family status, but you are old enough now to know that you—not the order in which you made your entrance into the world—are in charge of your actions and your destiny.

It does not matter what a person's birth order is, or who he or she has become; it is important to accept each person for who he or she is as an individual. We cannot form an opinion about people we know because they fit into certain categories such as "firstborn" or "only child." With that being said, there are some common threads that often appear in an individual's personality or sibling relationships, relating to his/her birth order.

The eldest child does receive the most attention from her/his parents during those early years. If the family is healthy and loving and their focus is on learning, then this often means that the oldest child will be more advanced and the most capable of taking on additional responsibilities. The eldest often feels responsible and is often more successful than the other siblings.

Also, the eldest often has the highest expectations and the toughest rules placed on him/her. The eldest children are the ground breakers. The expectations are higher for the eldest child. Parents usually relax a bit on the later children because they have a better idea of what to expect from the child and the attention given to the children has to be shared. Because the expectations are higher for the eldest child, these characteristics are retained and the oldest child may continue to have high expectations of them and of what "right behavior" looks like. Eldest children are often caretakers, especially in healthy, loving households.

The next-oldest child often shares many of the responsibilities, but does not have the drive or the special privileges that the oldest child receives. The oldest is usually seen as the smartest—when the second child is not. The second child is not seen as the oldest, or the smartest; he/she often feels left out. This child and the eldest child are often competing with each other to prove his or her accomplishments, or the perceived expectations. The second-oldest may go out of his/her way to be different from the eldest; he/she may give up or simply shut down. Siblings who are close together in age often take one of two routes: either they are best friends and share everything, or they do not get along at all.

The oldest child tends to control the relationship; he/she enjoys being able to control the other child or will work hard to keep his/her best friend. The role the oldest child assumes can depend on the parent(s) and how they treat both children. The parent(s) can also teach the children to care for each other. If the parent(s) are loving and respectful toward each other and toward the children, then the children will model that behavior. There are times when the eldest child will enjoy the role as a surrogate parent and can cause a lot of conflict between other members of the family. If the oldest child feels as though he/she is in danger of losing his/her leadership role in the family, then he/she may work hard to maintain that position and further dominate the other children in the family.

Many times, the second child can feel very inadequate and become angry at and defiant with other family members. That second-oldest may feel as though he/she will never possess the same skills as the oldest child—nothing ever seems to be good enough. Sometimes the younger siblings spend a lifetime trying to measure up to the standards of others. The younger children can be in for a rude awakening when they are finally in the place to make decisions and have more control in the family—only to discover that having this power is not what they expected.

When there are three children in the family, the youngest child wants everyone to be happy and get along, and will sometimes try to make other members of the family laugh. They are often uncomfortable with conflict in the home. They tend to be peacemakers; they will act the clown in order to get attention and to make others happy. The youngest child in a family often gets more attention during the critical formative years because there is no new baby to "replace" him or her.

Also, for each additional child, the parents tend to make differences in the way the children are treated. This can cause problems because the children will begin to notice and complain about it. The children will notice that the rules have changed. They are more relaxed for the younger children and older children, depending on the time and activity in which they want to participate. This can cause conflict between youngest and older siblings (who feel that the youngest has it easy and is "spoiled"). There may be some jealousy about the amount of attention that the youngest child receives. This can translate into rougher treatment for the younger children—given by the older siblings. Older children may feel as though the youngest child gets all the attention and love from the parents; therefore, the oldest child will not give the youngest child needed attention.

There were times when my older sisters acted as my protector and tried to keep me from being caught in situations that would bring harm to me, and there were times when they felt that I received more attention than they did. There were many times when I felt left out and had to struggle to get "my share" of the attention. One's growing up in a large family can possibly make him/her easily feel left out of the main stream.

Older children tend to be very protective and enjoy spending time with the younger siblings. When the older siblings attend the same school as the younger siblings, they will take care of the younger siblings by bringing them along for their own activities. They may be exposed to the fun things that can teach the younger child things that are helpful—and things that they are not ready for as well. This treatment often does result in a spoiled youngest.

The youngest child in a family who is born several years after the others can be every bit as spoiled; many times they are over-pampered. They do not understand the difference between their childhood and those of the older children's. Different treatment shown to this youngest may be the result of parents' usually having more money later in life, or providing things to the oldest child and not being as generous with the younger child. The youngest children may receive more financial assistance and expensive gifts (a car, money for college, and so forth) that were not available to older children—or it could be the opposite. I often hear statements made by my daughter about how the treatment she received was different from that of her older brother's. This reality can result in sibling jealousy.

Of course, the other side of the sibling story is that the youngest can become a people pleaser and know how to make others happy. He or she is someone who does not like conflict and is good at getting what he/she wants. In a home where there is conflict, the youngest may not have received adequate attention as a young child should. Many times the parents may have been too busy trying to solve their own problems and failed to give the child the needed attention. This circumstance may cause the child to be venerable to anyone who shows him/her love or gives him/her positive attention. For example, when young girls do not get the love and attention they need at home, they may look for that love and/or that relationship with older boys and men.

In a home where there is conflict, children often become closer in order to survive the abuses from their parents. They look out for each other for support. The oldest child may resort to behavior such as drinking, drugs, self-mutilation, early sexual activity, and other unhealthy activities. This child looks for ways to cope with his/her pain also. This eldest child is likely to get married early—in her search for a more loving relationship. She may find a way to move away from the family in order to escape the pain of the past. This is a means of coping with what she has experienced. She will try to remove herself form anything that reminds her of her past painful experiences—which may include her younger siblings.

These descriptions present common behaviors and traits—and we must not forget that each person is unique and copes with challenges in his/her own way. Children must understand that parents have problems and they cope with those problems in different ways. They must also understand that their parents' behavior is just that: "their parents' bad behavior"; and it is not their fault that their parents react in undesirable ways. They can maintain healthy and supportive sibling relationships as adults.

It is common for each child in a family to go through some period of withdrawal from the family dynamics. Each of us has a desire to find self, and to define who "me" is, without the expectations of the family that has known us to be a certain way our whole lives. This withdrawal can happen at any time in our lives: in the midst of our teenage years, during the first year of marriage, or any time in between. It can happen at any time when we have had a chance to ponder who we are when no one else is around. There are times when people will say, "I need time for me." This statement is true; there are times when all of us need time alone.

After graduating from high school and being at home (with other siblings being away at school or married), being at home was quite lonely for me. I was planning to attend college and realized that life could be very scary. I was afraid because I had to make choices on my own and I was leaving home for the first time. Temporary withdrawal was a time for me to question my religious beliefs, my moral values, my future, or other lifestyle choices. I had to look closely at my beliefs and how I would interact with others.

In our doing this evaluation of ourselves and our lives, once we know who and what we are, it is much easier to feel more comfortable with the family and establish positive and loving, mature sibling relationships. In the end, this is all that really matters in our lives. Our personal relationships define us and show who we really are. And it is about more than the money, our careers, our lifestyles—it is about how we treat people.

As in all life situations, our traveling on rocky roads and making U-turns can derail us. In the following chapter, take a look at some of the stresses that accompany family life and, as a result, our relationships with our mothers, daughters, sisters, and friends.

# Chapter Three

# Stress in the Family

*"The family. We were a strange little band of characters
trudging through life sharing diseases and toothpaste,
coveting one another's desserts, hiding shampoo,
borrowing money, locking each other out of our rooms,
inflicting pain and kissing to heal it in the same instant,
loving, laughing, defending, and trying to figure out
the common thread that bound us all together."*
~Erma Bombeck

Erma Bombeck's above quote clearly illustrates what it was like for me—living with my mother, my daughter, and my sisters. My family was a strange little band of characters, co-existing in our own little world. Sometimes, I wonder how families ever survived those little everyday arguments and fights:

*"Mom, she tore a hole in my blouse!"*
*"Mom, Ann won't let me have the hairspray!"*
*"Mom, Dianne won't get out of the bathroom!"*
*"Mom, she got the last piece of cake and I didn't get any!"*
*"Mom, why can't I go with my sisters to the park? I'm old enough to take care of myself!"*

When we are children, every little incident can be a big deal…and it does not matter how trivial the problem is, it can cause stress in the family. Stress exists in life. We cannot avoid it; it does not matter how rich we are, how beautiful we are, whether we are firstborn children, middle-born children, or the youngest in our families…stress exists. It can be more difficult for the children who grow up in single-parent homes; the stresses of day-to-day living—such as handling the bills, chores, and family activities in general—are likely amplified. And we cannot avoid the crises that occur. However, learning to cope with daily family stress can strengthen your family and make it easier for you to cope with family crises as well.

Communication is very important. Being available to talk to one another is the key to overcoming those crises which inevitably will arise. And because we live in a time when there are single-parent homes and many times both partners in a family have careers and children are involved in diverse extracurricular activities, it is very easy for the family unit to break down—resulting in a number of separate individuals living under one roof. Each individual can become isolated, facing his/her own problems and left to solve them on his/her own. That can be very stressful for the individual trying to solve his/her own problems. The family unit needs to be strong and should work together, in order for the solution to be effective.

Stress is natural, and it is unavoidable; however, it is important for all family members to understand stress and know how to deal with it effectively. Understanding that stress can and will affect all family members can help you do a better job of dealing with stressful situations in the family; however, there are times when situations that are stressful for one person may have very little effect on another person.

When considering families that experience a great deal of stress, it was found that these families became stronger because of the stress. It was also found that the individuals and families that were studied became stronger as they experienced the stressful events in their lives. They were able to work through the stressful situations successfully—therefore developing a greater appreciation for the calm periods in their lives, and many times learning powerful lessons because of the stressful situations.

In our society, things change rapidly—and with change comes stress. Today's family structure is undergoing many changes. If you are like the average person today, you have more than one hundred or more unread e-mails full of business advice, learning opportunities, and cyber issues to deal with each day. Our world is cluttered and difficult to manage; this causes a great deal of stress for all members of the family. Stress can kill your spirit; it can make you ill. It kills your motivation to get up in the morning and face another day. It can quite literally kill you.

One facet of life that can be stressful is marriage. Being a mother, daughter, and/or sister can be stressful. As for the institution of marriage, it can be a strong, supportive force that helps family members cope with family issues. However, a large number of marriages end in divorce, and many children will spend part of their lives with only one parent. Learning to deal with these changes creates opportunities for families to become stronger—or they can become weakened and less able to cope.

All families go through various stages of stress. The birth of a child places new demands on the family—as well as the death of a close family member, or even the loss of a pet. And teenagers' attempts to make their own decisions can lead to stress between the parent and the teenager as well. Often the most stressful times occur when a family experiences a variety of demanding events, one after the other. There are times when serious, isolated stressful events pile up; these should be the times when the family works together—which could mean getting outside help in order to do so. It is the flexible and practical family that meets the challenge of stress head-on and is able to adapt to changes that will produce a positive outcome. Family communication is the key to coping with stressful times.

The events retold in the following account were a source of stress for me: One incident that I remember well is when my sisters and I had to take turns washing the dishes. In my mind, it was never clear whose turn it was to wash the dishes. My youngest sister never had a turn. I felt that it was not fair. This was a big deal for my family; it caused stress for me and other family members. I was punished whenever I refused to wash the dishes because I felt that it was not my time to wash them. I would ponder, *why doesn't she have to wash dishes?* And as trivial as the matter of taking turns washing dishes seems to be, I remember it as being a very big deal for me and something I remember to this day. (And as you are read this account, you will most likely remember something that happened in your life that was very stressful for you.)

Another source of stress for me was when my oldest sister would constantly tell me what to do. I can profess that I was never comfortable with it. I mean, *who made her the boss?* As a woman, I now realize that an older family member—like a sister—is given responsibilities that the younger siblings do not have.

My older sister was not given instructions on how to be a surrogate mother, but often, that is what she was. She did the best with what she knew without anyone giving her instructions on how to do what she did. No one told her how to be a second mother; therefore, she did what she was told the best way she knew how. She knew that her job was to take care of the younger siblings. *I love you for this now, dear sister!*

Needless to say, family togetherness does not translate into constantly holding hands. It does not mean that all people are treated equally and have to do their share of the chores. You can be conscious of the fact that daily family stress can build strong families that can weather both small storms and large crises. Example: Just because Dad and Jimmy like football does not mean that Mom and Lorraine have to like it, too. The phrase "quality time" has become trite with overuse, but it is quality time spent together that matters. The following are a few ideas that can help alleviate stress and, as a result, help you to become a better mother, daughter, sister, and friend (not to overlook fathers and sons):

1.  ***Schedule household chores.*** Assigning duties to each family member can make the house run smoothly. When each family member knows what is expected of him/her, there should be less confusion. Involving all family members in the plan can give everyone ownership.

2.  ***Share a meal; share at least one meal each day.*** Sharing a meal gives the family a time to come together and discuss what their successes are—as well as their concerns. If you cannot do it every day, schedule it as a regular family "event." This is a great way to learn about what other family members are doing.

3.  ***Plan family events.*** A special activity can be as simple as a trip to the local park—or just a family movie night. Make a list of movies that you all want to see. Give each family member an opportunity to share his/her ideas. Then, choose one of them and schedule a specific night and time for the event. Let everyone know that his/her ideas are important and perhaps can be done all at the same time or each at a different time. Each family member will choose what he/she will be responsible for.

4.  ***Have a board game night.*** With all the video games and online games, some people have forgotten how to sit with each other and play good old-fashioned board games. Video games are fine, however. The Scrabble™ game or

28

Monopoly™ game can challenge the family members to take a closer look at the other family members. Emphasize the fact that the family is playing a game together—therefore, it is not always important to win. Schedule this game night once a week, if possible. There is no better way to reconnect with your family members and even with friends!

### *Managing Family Stress*

A strong family unit develops the tools to solve problems, thus reducing stress for the entire family. And if you have the tools to solve family stressors, then you will have the tools to nurture your relationships as a mother, daughter, sister, or friend.

Stresses in the family can carry over to the whole family (such as school suspensions, addictions, mental disorders, or physical illnesses)—or family crises (such as a death in the family, financial problems, storms, or a fire).

When managing individual stressors that affect the family, keep a few tips in mind:

1. ***Be open for discussion.*** If it is a problem for you or a problem that you notice is stressing out another family member, chances are that it is a stressor for the entire family as well. Talk it out and work toward finding a solution.
2. ***Don't downplay stressful situations.*** No matter what the problem is, find time to listen to the person who is most affected by the problem. Let the individual talk it out, be a good listener, and show him/her that solving the problem is important to the family. Let others weigh in on how the problem can be solved.
3. ***Don't lay blame.*** When there is a problem, it really does not matter who is at fault. Define the problem and work toward a solution.
4. ***Respect the privacy of others.*** If a family member tells you something in confidence, respect it. Do not disclose the information to others without having discussed this with the person. If you are unable to agree to keep the confidence, then be honest with him/her.

In concluding this section, it is important to know that building a strong family unit reduces stress for all family members and effectively managing day-to-day stress not only makes one's home a place for each member to relax and recharge, but also builds the skills necessary for the family to come together in a crisis and effectively manage family stress.

### Being a Mother—a Parent

As a mother, I realize that from the monster under the bed for small children to the stress of taking the SATs and final exams for the college-bound, stress affects kids of all ages. The first thing a parent can do to help his/her child manage stress is to build a strong family unit. Parents should include their children in family discussions and be on the lookout for stress that is affecting their kids.

Small children with underdeveloped communication skills may display stress very differently than adults do. Often kids' stress is internalized and most noticeable in physical symptoms—such as when they exhibit frequent flu-like symptoms, including headaches, stomachaches, and even nausea. Children under stress may regress to behaviors like bedwetting and frequent crying. A normally active child becomes either less active or hyperactive; a usually quiet child has fits of anger; or a child who often "acts out" becomes very quiet.

Some signs of stress in kids are easily confused with other problems. For instance, if a child's schoolwork slides or there is a change in his/her circle of friends, this might be taken to mean that something else is wrong (other than what is claimed to actually be wrong). The changes may simply indicate a child's inability to handle a stressful situation. Recognizing the stress and working to provide a calm environment will work wonders for all of the family members.

In our society, it is fine for us to experience work-related stress, but not family-related stress. When we "buy into" these unrealistic expectations, we are sure to be disappointed. The truth is that most families fall short of this ideal view.

A certain amount of family stress is inevitable. It is how a family handles stress that is important. Families can develop effective coping skills for handling stress. Probably the best way is through the individual communication and family reactions to situations. Families under stress may report some of the following:

- Little time to spend together.
- A desire for the simpler life.
- There is never time to relax.
- Constant conflict.
- Arguments.
- Engaging in meaningless conversations.
- Always tense.

When there is less stress in the family, there is time to enjoy and support each other, communicate with each other, set priorities, and view stress as a challenge that is both temporary and controllable. It is never too late to learn coping strategies.

- ***Vigorous exercise is a good stress reliever.*** All of us need a period to unwind. Encourage your children to get on their feet and keep moving and engage in activities like biking, volleyball, and other activities that will keep one on his/her feet. Whenever your child appears to be stressed, make it a point to play an active game, such as kickball or volleyball; go for a walk and take time to talk. Time spent with your kids is a great vehicle for getting them to open up the lines of communication.
- ***Be clear in setting rules, and consistent with discipline.*** Kids live in a "black-and-white" world. Never blur the rules and always be consistent.
- ***Show affection by hugging and complimenting your child.*** Sometimes a hug is worth more than a thousand words. Give your child a gentle massage on the neck and shoulders.
- ***Be a good listener.*** When your child wants to talk about his or her problems, do not criticize. Listen and give advice, if need be. Giving advice is not always necessary. Encouraging words are always good medicine.
- ***Help your kids understand that everyone makes mistakes.*** A good start is admitting your mistakes to your children with an "I'm sorry." Even if you were unsuccessful in dealing with your situation, you will teach your kids that you can learn from and even laugh at your own mistakes.
- ***Finally, teach your kids stress-relieving exercises and help them find stress-reducing games they can play to reduce their stress.***

The following list of strategies can help produce a less-stressful household, and allow more time for interaction among family members:
- Make lists.
- Be realistic about time objectives.
- Let go of strict timelines.
- Accept that there will always be different issues to face.
- Change chores, if necessary.
- Purchase goods and services that you can afford.
- Let go of the "I have to control everything" attitude.
- Be thankful for small accomplishments.

- Acknowledge small acknowledgments.
- Say no to things that are not important to you.
- Learn to say yes to things in which your child is directly involved.
- Try not to spread yourself too thin.
- Limit time spent on the telephone.
- If it doesn't feel right, then it's not for you.
- Learn to leave unnecessary things behind.
  (Refer to http://www.usbanext.uiuc.edu/)

### A Personal Offering

For all mothers out there—for all sisters, daughters, and friends—I have put together a personal list of activities for you *(just for you)* in order to help you de-stress from the hectic, everyday life that has become the "norm."

### Listen to Soft Music

Whenever you are feeling overwhelmed by a stressful situation, try taking a break and listening to relaxing music, reading, exercising, or engaging in other activities that help you stay calm. Playing calm music has a positive effect on the brain and body, and can help lower blood pressure and reduce cortisol. I recommend listening to the kind of music that you enjoy. Classical is good; however, if classical really is not your thing, then try listening to ocean or nature sounds—something that is slow and soothing…something that will help produce similar relaxing effects to music. Or, if you have some personal music of your own that brings you peace and joy, by all means, listen to it!

### Discuss Unpleasant Situations with a Friend

Whenever you are feeling overwhelmed, take a break and call a friend so that you can talk about your problems. Talk to someone whom you trust. Not only do you want good relationships with your mother, daughter(s), and sister(s), but you also want to nurture good relationships with your friends. Good relationships with friends and loved ones are important to any healthy lifestyle—and there is no time when this is more evident than when you are under a lot of stress. A reassuring voice, even for a minute, can put everything in perspective.

### Keep a Journal

Sometimes calling a friend is not an option. If this is the case, then talking to *you* can be the next best thing to avoid becoming too stressed out. Do not worry about feeling crazy; just tell yourself the reason why you are stressed out, what you have to do to complete the task at hand, and, most importantly, that everything will be okay. If you prefer, write a letter to yourself or write in your journal in order to help you sort out your thoughts and relieve stress.

### Take a Walk

For many of us, the best thoughts come in the morning after waking—while still in bed. I love walking and exercising every morning. It is a great way for me to reconnect with myself, clear my mind, problem solve, and just enjoy the solitude of the day.

### Eat Healthy Foods

Stress levels and a proper diet are closely related. Fruits and vegetables are always good, as is fish with high levels of omega-3 fatty acids, which have been shown to reduce the symptoms of stress. A tuna sandwich really is brain food. Sometimes we forget to eat well and, instead, resort to indulging in sugary, fatty snack foods or fast foods from a drive-thru as a pick-me-up. Try to avoid the vending machine and drive-thru.

### Take a Deep Breath

Take about five minutes out of your day to exercise; sit up in your chair with your feet flat on the floor, with your eyes closed and your hands on top of your knees. Breathe in and out slowly and deeply, concentrating on your lungs as they expand fully in your chest. Count slowly from ten to one. Take deep breaths to oxygenate your blood. This helps center your body, and clears your mind.

### Take Time to Laugh

Laughter releases endorphins that improve mood and decrease levels of the stress-inducing hormones *cortisol* and *adrenaline*. The theory that "laughter is the best medicine" applies to all of us. Rent a comedy movie and watch it on your television as often as possible.

### Drink Hot or Warm Tea

While many people rely on the stimulating effects of coffee, it is important to note that caffeine does increase blood pressure. In other words, caffeine stresses you out. Instead of coffee or energy drinks, try green tea or chamomile tea. It has less than half the caffeine of coffee and contains healthy antioxidants, as well as thiamine—an amino acid that has a calming and soothing effect on the nervous system.

### *Meditate*

While most of the tips I have suggested provide immediate relief, there are also many lifestyle changes that can be more effective in the long run. The concept of "meditation" is a large part of somatic approaches to mental health and has become en vogue in psychotherapy. From Yoga and Tai Chi to meditation, these mental exercises may prevent stress from becoming a problem in the first place. Take an exercise or dance class. Find stress-reducing exercises on the Internet.

### *Exercise Daily*

Exercising does not necessarily mean power lifting at the gym or training for a marathon. A short walk around the office or simply standing up to stretch during a break at work can offer immediate relief in a stressful situation. Getting your blood circulating releases endorphins and can improve your mood almost instantly.

### *Get Enough Sleep*

Everyone knows that stress can cause one to lose sleep—and a lack of sleep is also a key cause of stress. This vicious cycle causes the brain and body to get out of sync and only gets worse and worse with time. Make it a point to get the doctor-recommended seven to eight hours of sleep. Turn the TV off earlier and do your best to get into bed at a reasonable time. It may be the most effective way to get rid of stress.

### *Learn More about Stress Relief*

Stress is an unavoidable part of life—but that does not mean that you should ignore it. Too much untreated stress can cause serious physical and mental health problems.

The good news is that you can manage stress. With some patience and a few useful strategies, you can reduce your stress—whether it is family stress or stress at the workplace. Stress is just a part of life, and we have to learn to manage it.

# *Chapter Four*

# What It Means to Be a Daughter

*"You don't choose your family.
They are God's gift to you, as you are to them."*
~Bishop Desmond Tutu

Before I was a mother, I was a daughter. Being a daughter taught me how to become a better mother to my own daughter. Every day that goes by equips me to know and understand my mother better. I tried to show appreciation for our mother when she was with us. I did not wait for Mother's Day to honor her with gifts, helping her clean, or just laughing on the phone...if I saw something that I knew she would like—such as a blouse or shoes or a dress—I would buy it for her. I wanted her to know how much I appreciated her.

That trend carried over to my children—who were given as much as I could afford to give them. I must confess that there were times in my childhood when I did not feel appreciated as much as I thought I should have been—especially in my teenage years. As I look back, I know that the teens can be difficult years for all of us. As with many teens, I felt as  though my friends had more freedom than I did. I would get a little upset when my mom would not let me go out with friends. I used to envy my girlfriends, whose parents (I felt) gave them the freedom to do things that I could not do. But **now**, as I look back, I really appreciate what my parents did and how they loved me and protected me. I did not appreciate it at the time, but I really understand their wisdom and decisions that were made in my best interest.

A Daughter is just a little girl who grows up to be your best friend

There were times when I could not wait to grow up and take charge of my life and do the things that I wanted to do. I really did not like for anyone to tell me what to do—and that included being told what to do by my mother and father. As an adult, I look back and realize how fortunate I was to have parents who cared enough to protect me the way they did. It was important to give my children that same sense of security.

When I became a mother, I realized that there can and will be many times when mothers and daughters will have their differences. Mothers and daughters are usually alike in many ways: in personality, body language, gestures, and so forth. This is usually the case because of two reasons: the first being because the daughter is raised by her mom, and the second is because the daughter will naturally carry some of her mother's personality traits and actions. This makes for a very special motherhood bond. Most mothers and daughters can be best friends as the daughter becomes a young adult (but not always), because a mother-daughter love naturally makes for a lot of the same interests, and at times can cause conflict between the two of them. Even though my daughter and I have our differences, we love each other and really enjoy being together. Our roles have changed and she is a wonderful and wise young lady. I realize that she is capable of making good decisions—therefore, I listen to her and many times take her advice.

When mothers and daughters have a good relationship and love each other, that can make everything okay—when you are a child or an adult. And mothers get a great deal of satisfaction out of helping daughters and sons out of difficult situations. Whether it is a wound or a broken heart, nothing seems to be too big for Mom to fix. A daughter puts a lot of faith and belief in her mom that she can  make everything better. I know I felt that way as a child. There is a strong sense of trust between them, which is what creates such a close, warm bond.

Another reason why mother-daughter love is so strong is because each depends on one another. The daughter depends on her mother because she has emotional and other developmental needs that only her mother can fulfill. In a general sense, a mother is always there for her daughter, no matter what happens. (Of course, as with everything, there are exceptions to this rule.) A mother generally accepts her daughter unconditionally and provides all the love necessary to make sure that she grows up to be a happy and well-rounded individual.

Mothers depend on their daughters from the moment their little bundle of joy is born. Mothers see their daughters as being an extension of them. Mother-daughter love can mean that a mother needs her daughter (or son) in order to feel complete. To a daughter, there is no greater person than her mother. Both mother and daughter help one another stay on the right path and experience a kind of happiness not easily found anywhere else. Their bond is most often untouchable and unbreakable. In the perfect scenario, they can talk to each other about anything and are truly best friends. When it is "right," there is nothing quite like mother-daughter love. It is the most special bond in the universe. Of course, there are relationships between some mothers and daughters that are not always "desirable."

In her groundbreaking book, *You Just Don't Understand: Women and Men in Conversation*, Deborah Tannen provides some insights into mother-and-daughter relationships. She asks this question: *Why do our mothers always criticize us? And why do we care so much?*

Deborah, 61, a professor of linguistics, explains that at the time she started writing her book, *You're Wearing That? Understanding Mothers and Daughters in Conversation,* she did not have a good relationship with her mom and wanted to know why. Unfortunately, her mother died while she was doing the research for the book. In her words, she admitted that she adored her mother, but she also admitted that her mother drove her mad. She found that the more women she interviewed, the more she was relieved to discover that she was not alone. But it was a shock for her to discover that so many daughters felt the same.

As a school counselor, I realized that many middle and high school females had a less-than-desirable relationship with their mothers. This can be a difficult time for mother-daughter relationships. Daughters want to make their own decisions, and their mothers are trying to keep them from making mistakes. This time between mother and daughter can be like a tug-of-war.

Tannen also explains that most women's relationships with their mothers were/are like an "intense love affair": a relationship that is very loving and/or a relationship that can be very painful. From talking to many mothers and daughters and analyzing their conversations, she came to understand why we get it so wrong—and what we can do about it.

Tannen explained that the relationship between mothers and daughters is probably both the most exciting and the most painful a woman ever has. It is the source of the deepest love and deepest anger—even hate—that we ever experience. We as mothers and daughters can take a simple, everyday conversation and make it the best or the worst conversation we have ever had. If you nab some coveted handbag in the sale, your mother will be the first to share your excitement. But tell her you are on a diet and she cannot resist saying, "Make sure you keep it up." That is when you feel like hitting her. *Why does she have to throw those negative jabs at you? Right?*

You share every hope and dream with her. She knows you inside out and is supposed to be on your side—so why does she insist on making you feel like a failure? It is the same when she gets onto the topic of your hair and your clothes. According to Tannen, they are never quite right. But ask your mother why she is so critical and she will be horrified; she genuinely thinks she is only trying to help. This does not happen with sons, simply because with mothers and daughters, "We are brought face-to-face with reflections of ourselves—which forces us to confront who we are, who we want to be, and how we relate to others."

It often boils down to our sending and/or receiving mixed messages in conversation. Conversations between mothers and daughters can be soothing—or they can be painful. Mothers want to be accepted and admired by their daughters, and daughters want to be loved and admired by their mothers. When this does not happen, the relationship is compromised. We cement our relationships with talk and have endless opportunities to say the wrong thing during those "talks."

A girl's best friend is the person to whom she *tells* everything. A man's best friend is the person with whom he *does* everything. A man can play tennis with his friend every week and not know that he is getting divorced. Can you imagine that happening with a woman? That will most likely be the first discussion on the agenda for a mother-daughter, sister-sister, or friend-friend conversation over coffee.

Your mother is the one person on Earth with whom you will share your delight via telephoning and announcing, "I finally got that bedspread for the spare room." But as we tell our mothers everything, there is also more opportunity to be criticized. And there are three universal flashpoints: hair, clothes, and weight (and on a sublevel, sometimes career and husband/boyfriend choices).

So why on Earth do mothers feel the need to be so hypercritical? It is not just that they feel the urge to offer advice—a throwback from when we were young. It goes much deeper.

Mothers notice our every flaw because they are scrutinizing us just as deeply as they do themselves. We are their reflections. We are the "little mothers" in child form. One woman said that it was the biggest surprise of her life to discover that her daughter did not turn out exactly like her. Sons would have to dye their hair blue and wear it down to their waists before they came in for that same level of attention. Mothers simply do not pay as much attention to their sons because their sons are not reflections of them.

The irony for daughters is that the person we most want approval from is the one most likely to criticize us. Quite simply, if a woman did not love her mother so much, then she (the mother) would not have the power to hurt her *so much.* And if the mother did not love her daughter so much, then she would not notice her daughter's every fault, and want to improve it.

Most mothers try to be tactful. But we (as daughters) can always hear that underlying message. If your mother says, "Are you going to wear that?" you know that she really means, "That does not look good on you." So then you become angry—but only because you want her approval; then she claims that you are touchy. Keep this in mind: Understanding that your mother does not mean to hurt you can transform your relationship.

Mother-daughter relationships can be intense. If your mother was a housewife and you have a glittering career, she is probably very proud. But her pride is tempered by a sense of rejection and possibly envy. *Perhaps she wanted you to be a nurse and, instead, you are an executive in a huge corporation.* This can create a difference in communication.

When I was a young girl growing up in the south, my mom seldom worked outside the home (as mothers tend to do today). She was very supportive of my sisters and me and always wanted us to do well in whatever career path we decided to pursue. She was concerned that we would become involved in anything that would be harmful for us. She was also concerned and hoped that we would always make good choices when it came to our personal lives. When I went off to college, my mom wanted to know about the kind of people I had as my friends, and whom I was dating as well. She was strict but gave limited advice—sometimes unwanted advice.

It is for this very reason that we sometimes yearn for our own space. But trying to keep our mothers at an arm's length can make things even worse. It is like an endless seesaw, causing pain and confusion. When girls go away to college, many mothers ask for intimate details about their lives. When my mom questioned me, I thought she was interfering in my life; however, I eventually understood that she was concerned about me and the decisions that I made. She was looking for ways to give me good, sound advice. I realized that by refusing to talk about what was happening in my college life, I was driving a wedge between us.

We expect competition from our friends, but many women find it impossible to admit the obvious. Some mothers are every bit as competitive with their daughters because we are women. One forty-year-old woman said that she was walking down the road arm in arm with her mother when her mother suddenly said, "It's not fair that all the men are looking at you, not me." This woman—the mother—was sixty-five years old. Few mothers would express their feelings so frankly…but most feel them just like this sixty-five-year-old woman did.

It is easy to concentrate on the problems. But each woman out of the majority of the women I interviewed said that she had a much better relationship with her daughter than with her mother. We are more open with our daughters than mothers were a generation ago, because we are learning how to better communicate. And we are recognizing the personality traits that come with being a mother to a daughter. We are doing a better job of communicating with our daughters and we want to make continuing improvements in that area. We want our daughters to nurture well-rounded relationships with their own daughters, if they have any.

Yes, there comes a time when we want our own space and want to make our own decisions without interference from Mom and Dad. Trying to keep Mom at arm's length can cause problems and perhaps cause pain, confusion, and even anger. Living in your own space—your own apartment—can help in this situation. In every situation, however, the relationship between you and your mom can be fragile and needs constant care and nurturing in order to make it a good one.

One twenty-year-old woman summed it up this way: "I have the best conversations of my life with my mother. I also have the worst." No bond is stronger than the one between mother and daughter. We can either regard it as a ribbon that ties a beautiful gift, or a tie that binds and imprisons. In a nutshell, mothers and daughters find in each other the source of great comfort—but also of great pain. We talk to each other in better and worse ways than we talk to anyone else. And these extremes can coexist within the same daughter-mother pairs.

Two sisters were in an elevator in the hospital where their mother was nearing the end of her life. "How will you feel when she's gone?" one sister asked. The other replied, "One part of me feels: *How will I survive?* The other part feels: *I want to hear her criticize me now.*"

The part of a daughter that feels "How will I survive?" reflects a passionate connection and love that she has for her mother: Wanting to pick up the phone and talk at her will. Wanting to get her opinion or ask her a question. But the part that sees her mother as someone annoying can reflect the way her anger can flare when a rejection or a disapproving word causes great pain.

American popular culture either romanticizes or demonizes mothers. We ricochet between the sentiments of "Everything I ever accomplished I owe to my mother" and "Every problem I have in my life is my mother's fault." Both convictions are laden with powerful emotions.

As mothers, women grapple with these contradictions. The adoration they feel for their grown daughters, mixed with the sense of responsibility for their well-being, can be overwhelming. When mothers and daughters do not stay connected, the pain that they feel can also be overwhelming. The tug-of-war between family members can last for years—causing unavoidable problems.

A woman in her sixties expressed this: "I thought the problems that my daughter and I had when she was young would end when she became an adult and we would become friends and enjoy each other's company. But I found that I was getting older and things start to hurt, and on top of that, the complications with your daughter still exist."

As for me, my daughter and I have a beautiful relationship; however, there are times when I make statements that can offend my daughter, such as, "Are you going to wear that?" or, "Do you really like that dress?" Though I would apologize, she would still remind me that the statement was inappropriate.

Especially disappointing—and puzzling—is that hurt feelings and even arguments can be sparked by the smallest, seemingly insignificant remarks. Here is another example:

"Are you going to put that in the salad?" Anna heard her mother's voice as she was preparing a salad. Anna was not comfortable with that statement, but felt a need to respond. "Well, I was," she answered. Her mother realized what she had done: she had made her daughter very uncomfortable.

Sometimes as mothers we forget that our little girls grow up and do not always make the same decisions that we will make or have made. Anna's mother probably thought she had asked a question that was very trivial—but her daughter did not feel that way because she became tense when she heard the implication, *"You don't know what you're doing; I know better."*

When daughters react with annoyance or even anger in the smallest way (through seemingly innocent remarks), mothers get the feeling that talking to their daughters can be like walking on eggshells: they have to watch every word. This can cause friction between the two of them. A mother's questions and comments which seem to imply that a daughter should do things another way can spark an unfavorable response—because they bring into focus one of the most uncomfortable reactions between mother and daughter. The double meaning of *connection* and *control* becomes evident.

Many mothers and daughters are as close as any two people can be—but closeness means that both should consider how her actions will affect the other person…and this can make her feel as though she is no longer in control of her own life. Any word or action can be interpreted as a sign that the other person is trying to control her. This double meaning was emphasized by my daughter and me in the following analogy. We talk on the phone almost every day—sometimes two or three times a day. She enjoys it and so do I. There are times when she will skip a few days. I understand that she is married, she is busy, and she feels as though she had to loosen the bonds. I understand, but I still question why she does not call on some days. Sometimes the close bond can cause the daughter to feel that she does not have the control that she should have as an adult. The phrase "loosen the bonds" can have a double meaning of connection and control.

Small comments made by each can cause hurt: It can come across as a vote of inadequacy, or it can be annoying coming from anyone—but it is especially painful when it comes from the person whose opinion you value. Statements coming from your mother may seem small to her; however, the smallest remark can bring into focus the biggest question that exists in conversations between mothers and daughters.

When mothers' comments to daughters (or, for that matter, daughters' comments to mothers) seem to answer questions in the affirmative, it is

**Mother & Daughter**

deeply reassuring—all is right with the world. But when their words seem to imply that the answer is "No, there's something wrong with what you're doing," then mothers can make daughters feel uncomfortable and they start to doubt whether how they do things (and if who they are) is really okay.

The mother-daughter bond is a powerful one, and can shape our lives when it comes to who we love, family, and connections. It can make our lives better or worse. How we communicate with our daughters is key to how our daughters will communicate with others.

Dr. Linda Mintle says that it is possible to have a meaningful adult relationship with your mom. She says the mother-daughter relationship is the perfect arena to develop and practice relationship-building skills that form and shape every other relationship in a woman's life—because the mother-daughter bond is such a close one. It is so close, in fact, that one cannot just forgive and forget the past. The more she learns to make peace and find a meaningful connection with her mom, the richer her other relationships will be.

### Simple Effective Tips to Improve Mother-Daughter Relations
- Do not try to get others on your team. You decide how you feel without outside opinions.
- Change for yourself, not because someone else thinks you should or is pressuring you to change.
- Do not underestimate your mother's reaction. Although she may object to a change in the relationship, that does not mean that you are wrong to make the change.
- Keep your visits limited and focused. This helps you hold on to your own sense of self.
- Write out your thoughts in a letter and read and listen to what is said.

Once you have a better sense of yourself, you can learn to be more empathetic, be a better listener, and develop a greater appreciation for your mother and others as well. You can exercise better communication skills when discussing issues. You will be able to allow yourself to see a broader, more balanced view of who your mother is and was. All these tips will help you improve communication with your mom and help the two of you to interact in a way that is comfortable for both of you.

### *Having a Child of Your Own*

There are times when you have probably heard young people make statements about what they would do if "that was my child"—or express the sentiment that "my child would not do that because…" One big factor for many adult daughters is that when they have a child of their own, they will find that the story is not what they had envisioned.

According to Dr. Mintle, having a child or children of your own usually creates more empathy for mom. When an adult daughter begins to grasp what her mother went through and how tough parenting really can be, she can then begin to have more empathy for her mother, and forgiveness and acceptance can follow. My love and appreciation was realized after I had my daughter.

---

*My daughters and I have that "love-hate" relationship.
We might not agree on a lot of things, but we know
at the end of the day, we love each other.*

~Anonymous Online Blogger

---

Also found in the article "Mother-Daughter Relationships," this is what two women had to say: "As you become an adult, your mom's role is switching with yours. Whether it is due to age, health, finances, or culture, daughters are better equipped to take care of their moms these days. 'As mothers age, even as they develop health problems, we're seeing the mother-daughter relationship improve/change,'" says Karen Fingerman, an associate professor of child development and family studies at Purdue University, in West Lafayette, Indiana, and the author of *Mothers and Their Adult Daughters: Mixed Emotions, Enduring Bonds*. The child will begin to take on the leadership role and the mother will pay attention to the child and agree with her suggestions more than she had done in the past. There is a role reversal. "Daughters feel needed, mothers feel loved. Both sides come to accept the other for who she is and is more in tune with the other's strengths and weaknesses," says Fingerman.

"Passing the baton of authority is hard work. There's tension, as daughters are faced with demands and uncertainties, and mothers may feel they're getting help they don't need," Fingerman says.

According to Lee Sharkey, a daughter can make her mother feel more valued as she (the mother) becomes less dominant. So the daughter should spend time thinking and talking about the traditions and the values that they both share. This encourages the daughter to see her identity as critically and positively linked with her mother's, and can help preserve the mother's sense of importance.

No decision gets made without the other's approval, which can be both a blessing and a curse. For girls, sameness is equal to closeness. In mothers and daughters, that translates into regarding each other as yardsticks by which they measure themselves, examining where they overlap and differ. When things are harmonious, it is like the ultimate love affair: there is one person you can always count on.

With the pressure to be the same, it is tough to create boundaries. When opinions differ, the stress of trying to gain the other's approval (or feeling bad because she disapproves) can be overwhelming. A daughter has to understand that Mom is not responsible for her anymore, and a mother needs to realize that none of her daughter's wins are her own wins; none of her losses are her own losses.

These relationships are so intense because they are often driven by a fear of abandonment. If you are a daughter, then slowly build boundaries so that you do not create a chasm between you and your mother. Daughters should emphasize how deeply they value their mothers' opinions, and then make it clear that certain forthcoming decisions will be solo ones. So many women try to make their mothers agree with them, and that is not necessary—mostly because they love their daughters, regardless...and always will.

---

*"You love her, sometimes you hate her.*
*Sometimes she's the last person you want to see.*
*But she's the first one you call for advice.*
*That is the seesaw of feelings between*
*mothers and daughters."*

~Anonymous Online Blogger

---

# Chapter Five

# What It Means to Be a Sister

*"Is solace anywhere more comforting than in the arms of a sister?"*
~Alice Walker

I have three sisters. I love and respect all of them; however, there are times when we do not see things the same way. There are times when we have to agree to disagree. Sister relationships can be difficult. Relationships simply are not easy to manage—and sister relationships can be the most difficult to control.

I have two older sisters and one younger sister whom I deeply love and respect. However, as I look back, there were incidents that I would not care to describe. One in particular that I can recall is this: there were times throughout our childhood when we disagreed about who would do certain chores. There were times when I felt as though my younger sister did not do her fair share of the chores. You can probably recall times when you felt that you were treated unfairly. This was a constant problem for me; however, times changed and we accepted some of those changes.

You and your sisters may differ on most things, but you have a deep connection, nonetheless. Still, unlike the "best friends" relationship, an element of competition, similar to sibling rivalry, can exist. I have had this with my sisters, even though I love them and enjoy their company.

*Is this you?* You clearly like each other and there are qualities that you admire in your sister(s). You want to be like the other, and despite your age difference, you know one another well. As for me, I have always wanted to be myself.

As a middle child, I always wanted to be accepted for who I was/am. I never wanted to be what someone else wanted me to be. I wanted my own identity. I want to be me and not be defined by anyone else or anything else. But your not falling in line or agreeing with other family members can cause confusion and can cause conflict among you and your siblings. Many times you feel as though they do not understand you and you do not understand them.

Your relationship with your sister can be challenging, because (in most families) there will always be a sense of competition. There are always some competitive feelings in families and especially among sisters—but we can repress them; however, we do not always do that. Your being vocal about your feelings may cause hurt feelings and cause friction in the family.

Cambridge University psychologist Terri Apter has studied the extraordinary bonds that unite and divide sisters and has included this information in a groundbreaking book, entitled *The Sister Knot: Why We Fight, Why We're Jealous, and Why We'll Love Each Other No Matter What.* Apter told this story in her book. Her sister, Marion, a successful dermatologist, phoned her, and was very excited as she told her about her latest achievements at work. As she listened to her sister, on one hand she was excited—and on the other hand, very uncomfortable. Apter told her sister how thrilled she was—and a part of her did not like what she heard. "I was green with envy." Her success made me feel like a failure.

Apter wrote, "It all comes down to the knotty problem of being sisters." As Apter discovered during her research for her book, the relationship between sisters is one of the most complex there is. It shapes our relationships with others. In short, we play out the sisterly role with other women. If that sounds all sweetness and light, forget it. Our sisterly feelings are likely to be a seething mass of resentment, fear, and envy."

There is no doubt that there is something uniquely wonderful about the sisterly bond. I feel it with my sisters and I am sure you do, too. Your sister may be your best friend who will fight to the death for you; but she is also the one most likely to begrudge your success.

Psychologists have exhaustively investigated family relationships and their impact on shaping us. But until *The Sister Knot*, by Apter, no one has examined the intricate relationship between sisters. She interviewed seventy-six sets of sisters—aged from five to seventy-six—and the results were both shocking and fascinating. She started her research because she was fascinated by her feelings for her sister. She wanted to understand what lay at the root of their love-hate relationship.

Any girl who read *Little Women* probably wondered, *what on Earth is the matter with me? Why don't I adore my sister the way Jo adored her sister Beth?* Now I know. It boils down to rivalry: I want what she has. Interestingly, this has nothing to do with your place or birth order in the family.

As a teenager, you probably remember a sister constantly wanting to wear your clothes. She wanted to borrow your shoes, or borrow your earrings. Sometimes that can be very annoying. You may ask yourself, "What will she want next?" *The rivalry exists.*

Looking back, my parents were always fair to us…but that did not matter. At times, I felt as though my mom gave more attention to my younger sister. Sometimes, I would withdraw. I can remember a time when I hit my younger sister because I felt that she was able to do things that I was not allowed to do, yet receive little or no consequences for her actions. There was a time when I hit my sister and, when my mom tried to punish me for my behavior, I ran. I knew that I was not supposed to hit my sister. There was no good reason for it, except for the fact that she was getting more attention than I was—and I was jealous. It was as simple as that.

While talking to a friend recently, she expressed her occasional dislike for her own sister. Her older sister always felt a need to be more talented, smarter, prettier, and better at everything. She expressed that her oldest sister would take every ounce of love and attention from the two younger sisters and said this made her feel inferior to her. She said she had a need to be better than the other sisters in every aspect of their lives.

Our sister is our chief champion and greatest companion, but she is also our most deadly competitor; and while every child vies for attention and love from his/her parent, the competition between sisters can be painful and long-lasting. With a sister, the acts of competitiveness create relationships that can last a lifetime. Someone of the same sex who looks and acts like us is constantly fighting to be in a superior position to us and establish her own identity and personality. Sisters are constantly fighting for their position of authority in the family and in the world.

Sisters envy each other, just as friends envy each other. They want that which they envy about each other, and many times they want to become her, then they feel that they will be loved by the people who matter most. *If I don't have what I envy or don't become the sister or friend that I envy, then she will rob me of the love I want. And then no one will protect me and I won't matter to anyone.* Because of their insecurities, these feelings are manifested in you. Do you recall feeling this way?

Envy between brothers or friends is subtly different, because boys are more objective, less sensitive, and more goal-oriented. They may compete in activities—sports and "manly" things—but they are less sensitive when it comes to watching their parents with the other brothers.

For women, the rivalry can become all-consuming. Many times, women will become so consumed with trying to be better than their counterpart that they lose precious time that can be best served in developing herself. One woman who was interviewed in Apter's book said that she still "shudders" when she recalls the hatred she felt for her sister. As a sleepwalker, she was frightened that she would murder her—acting out the aggression she could control when she was awake. "I felt utterly repulsed by her," she said

WHO NEEDS THERAPY
I HAVE MY SISTER

in the book. "When we sat in the back seat of the car, I would look out of the window so I couldn't see her at all." It was obvious that she did not like her sister very much. She said she would kick her or kick the seat when sitting behind her in the car.

We all probably remember things that we did to our sister and the pain we inflicted on her. The simple truth is that, thanks to our sisters, we learn as tiny children exactly how to use our empathetic skills to torture each other. That feeling for many continues throughout our adult years.

Sisters know each other well—so they know exactly how to humiliate and embarrass each other. Another woman, now 27, recalled her outrage when she discovered that her sister, who was three years her junior, would be coming to "her" school. I did not want her at my school.

She tells the story of when she told her sister that anyone who went into the toilet at break time would never make any friends. This is what she relayed: "So she didn't go to the toilet all day. I ran home after school, knowing she was in no state to keep up with me, and when she cried and wet her pants I felt the most awful pleasure."

Of course, one of the cruelest ways to score points against a sister is to steal her boyfriends—something which is all too common. One woman in Apter's book, in her thirties, admitted that she regularly stole her older sister's boyfriends, just to prove she was as loveable and desirable.

"I never thought about whether I liked them or not," she said. "I just wanted what she had. I liked them simply because they liked her. My entire sense of what I was worth was related to what my sister was worth." This is often true with friends, too. Actions like this one prompted a good friend of mine—Tara Colman—to say, "When meeting new people, you treat your 'would-be' friend like an enemy until they prove to be your friend." I can say that it is better to be safe than sorry. You grow up and find that the scars of the past do not always heal. Even today, my sister cannot trust that I will not steal men from her. When her marriage broke up, she accused me of having an affair with her husband.

With time we learn that, even though our sister may be our competition, we are capable of being every bit as successful and happy as she is. But jealousy can run so deep that we never totally lose it. Sisterly envy is at the root of why women find it so hard to be supportive in the workplace. They will not even offer a helping hand to women who cannot possibly be any threat to them. Women at the top often act as though there is not enough room for anyone else. They will go out of their way to keep another woman from succeeding; it is a habit learned very early in life.

One woman in Apter's book said that she was acutely aware of how sibling tensions still affect her. The woman was twenty-five years old, but still struggled with a form of envy that bore all the hallmarks of the nursery or the playground.

"When a woman we will call Susan came to our company for the job interview, she immediately made me uncomfortable because she was attractive and very clearly very intelligent," she said. "I tried to be detached and professional, but how could I? I just felt blinded by the fact that she was a very pretty woman. She's the kind of woman my mother would love me to be or the kind of woman that I would like to be." This woman went on to explain that she could see her becoming the star of the boardroom while the other women would feel invisible.

This helps to explain why women are so critical of the way other women choose to live their lives. Sisters grow up comparing not just their appearance and skills, but their choices. And underlying the comparison is the fear: *Have I made the wrong choice myself?* That is why, at work, women do not just question whether another woman is going to oust them, but whether another woman has a better life. Again, her success does not threaten us in any rational sense. But we cannot help but to envy her—the way we envied our sisters.

As females, we have a love-hate relationship with our female friends. We model our behavior with them on the way we treated our sisters. So, if your friend gets a promotion at work, you will be thrilled for her, but part of you may also be envious. Her success does not threaten you, but nevertheless, you fear that her success will somehow diminish you.

Keep in mind that all sisters are different. While they are capable of bringing out the very worst in us, they also bring out the absolute best as well. And that is something quite special. Because they are our flesh and blood, we love to see them succeed and we share their pains. And no one can understand us or our problems the way a sister can.

Sisters are there when you really need them—most of the time. Rivalry between sisters is there, but parents can do a lot to help their girls grow up to be confident and secure. Many sisters are not happy with the way their parents label them throughout life. Instead of finding their own personalities and qualities, the parents might say, "Oh, she is the pretty one." And to describe another sister, the parents might say, "She is the smartest." Those statements can cause hurt feelings that can last a lifetime.

While sisters can be very envious of each other, it can be quite healthy. We learn about life and how to communicate with others—how to stand up for ourselves in the world.

I am a middle child with brothers and sisters. It has not always been fun and games with my sisters. I felt as though my sisters were not always happy with the attention that I received…just as I was not always happy with the attention that they received from our parents. *Jealous?* Maybe. If that is the case, it will happen.

One instance of sibling rivalry among my sisters and me, as young adults, occurred in part because I was the smallest of the sisters. My mom made the statement (as parents do), "Chris is the only daughter smaller that I am." I do not know whether my sisters heard the statement, but they were keenly aware that I was the smallest of the sisters—which probably fostered some animosity in them. The point is this: When our mother was in the hospital and having problems with her short-term memory, she highlighted the fact that I had always been "the smallest" among the sisters. It became clear that my sisters were not always comfortable with it.

We girls gathered together one day in my mom's hospital room. That day, after we walked in the room and stood around my mom's bed, my older sister said, "Mother, do you know who that is?"—while pointing at me standing to the side of the bed. I had a big smile on my face. *Surely mother knows who I am*, I thought.

Mom looked at me and, with a puzzled look on her face, said, "Chris? Well…" she hesitated, "it *looks* like Chris, but it can't be. She's too fat for Chris. When did she gain all that weight?" My sisters had a good laugh because I was finally told that I was no longer the "small sister." Jealousy? Well, it does exist in families—but it does not have to cause friction.

My sisters and I get along well, and I know that even when we are ancient, my older sisters will probably still tell me to put my coat on when it is cold, and I still will not be happy when they tell me what I should do and what I should not do. But underneath it all, we know we do it because we love each other…and we always will.

# *Chapter Six*

# What It Means
# to Be a Mother

*"When you are a mother,
you are never really alone in your thoughts.
A mother always has to think twice,
once for herself and once for her child."*
~Sophia Loren

### Women and Beauty

*"Do your eyes light up when they walk into the room?"*
~Toni Morrison

Remember that all of us want to feel validated and all of us want to feel that we are special. With that being said, when your child enters the room, put the paper down. Stop what you are doing. Consider that time as "sacred time." Use that time to acknowledge your child's strengths and treat your child as though he or she is the most precious person in the world to you. Ask yourself, "Do my eyes light up when my child enters the room?"

As with every day, I am excited about the *new* day. There are many possibilities for me, for my children, and for my grandchildren. Being a mother creates a whole new paradigm of possibilities.

Though I am over forty years old, I am still learning from things that my mother taught me. I think that as I continue to grow, I will better understand more of all that she taught me. I hope that in some magnificent or small way I can do the same for my children.

My mother taught me how to become a woman of strength and I want that for my daughter and granddaughter—because we need strong women (and men) in this world. Even though it is the twenty-first century, there are times when I think our world goes backwards instead of forward when it comes to women's equality. (But that is another topic for another book.)

Women are still behind in many facets of life. When I was a young girl, I thought that marriages were all made in heaven. But after being a counselor, wife, and mother myself, I realize that marriages are made "on Earth"—with all the problems that come with being on Earth. The fact that birth order plays a role in our marriages and in our roles as mothers is often overlooked. First, let us take a look at what it means to be a mother, in and of itself.

As mothers, we are the #1 person in our homes, in our husbands' and daughters' lives—our children's lives; this is something that always has been and always will be (in most cases)…because this is the position in which God has placed us. There are definitely times when this can be a very difficult position to be in.

Being a mother is not easy. I like to think of motherhood as sitting back, relaxing, and watching my little, perfect children play around me. The children are all sweet and loving. They get along well with one another and are model children. They make their beds, make all A's in school, and play games in a calm and orderly manner; they play their video games together. You might be laughing right now because, of course, this is not a realistic scenario. These idyllic moments might happen in brief periods of time, but they are not things that happen every day or every night. Maybe they *seldom* happen in your household—and the reason is because children are people, too; and none of us is perfect.

First, if you are a woman (and probably most of you reading this book are women— although men could learn a lot if they would read it), then you began life as a daughter yourself. Then, you might have progressed to being a sister…if you are lucky enough to have other siblings. Then you grew up and got married—and now it is your turn to be a parent: a mother.

The transition into parenthood is not always an easy task. The transition into motherhood, as well as the time spent getting to know your baby, are ongoing processes. Once you have healed from the birth of your child and you are feeling more rested, have developed a sense of confidence in being able to care for your baby, and have fallen in love with your baby, you will come to the realization that life will be different.

You will likely experience some or all of the following emotions/ feelings:

- Loss of control;
- Frustration and/or anger;
- Anxiety and uncertainty;
- Being overwhelmed; and,
- Mental and/or physical exhaustion.

You must not worry too much; just know that these feelings are all a normal part of the transition into parenthood. In the process of adjustment, you will later come to feel more "in control" of things; you will have more energy and will reach the point of being better adjusted emotionally as well.

This part of the transition into parenthood is where you are working to actively rebuild your day-to-day life—with focus on your new family.

During this stage of the transition into parenthood, you are doing these things:

- Focusing on making conscious decisions about your activities and your day-to-day life;
- Focusing on regaining a sense of control over your routines and daily life, and on feeling better; and,
- Making decisions about work and/or returning to work.

As you are adjusting and you proceed through the process of adjusting to your new roles and responsibilities, and to knowing what is important and what is not, eventually you will feel as though things are finally "back to normal" and you will also feel like "yourself" again. Life will be different—for you will have found a new "normal" and you will establish a new routine…and you will adjust to the new routine. For some moms, it takes less time; for others, it takes longer.

The transition into parenthood can be a difficult process—but it does not have to be. There are a number of very important resources that can help mothers make this as smooth a process as possible. They are the same resources that help to prevent postpartum depression.

### Baby Blues

When I was a new mother myself, no one had warned me about postpartum depression...or the *Baby Blues,* as it is sometimes called. Some of my friends have experienced this—some more than others. Approximately 80 percent of women experience something called the baby blues: feelings of sadness and emotional surges that begin in the first days after childbirth. In the throes of the baby blues, a woman might feel happy one minute and tearful and very emotional  the next. She might feel sad, blue, irritable, discouraged, unhappy, tired, or moody. Baby blues can be short-lived or can last for a relatively long period of time.

Being emotional at this time is believed to be a natural effect of the hormone shifts that occur with pregnancy and childbirth. Levels of estrogen and progesterone that increased during pregnancy drop suddenly after delivery; and this can affect one's mood. These female hormones return to their pre-pregnancy levels within a week or so—but we know that if one is dealing with lots of extra weight then this can add to the depression. Getting proper rest, nutrition, and support are quite important.

All experts agree that to cope with baby blues, new moms should try to accept help in the first days and weeks after labor and delivery. Let family and friends help with errands, food shopping, household chores, or child care. Let someone prepare a meal or watch the baby while you relax with a shower, a bath, or a nap. I know all of this *is not always possible,* but take as much time as you can in order to care for yourself while you are caring for others.

The experts also tout this: Getting plenty of rest and eating nutritious foods are important. Talking to people close to you, or to other new mothers, can help you feel supported and remind you that you are not alone. You do not have to stifle the tears if you feel the need to cry a bit—but try not to dwell on sad thoughts.

For some women, the feelings of sadness or exhaustion run deeper and last longer than baby blues. About 10 percent of new mothers experience postpartum depression. Postpartum depression is a true clinical depression triggered by childbirth—which usually begins two to three weeks after giving birth, but can start any time within the first few days, weeks, or months of post-delivery.

A woman with postpartum depression may feel sad, tearful, discouraged, hopeless, worthless, or alone. She also may experience the following:

- Trouble concentrating or completing routine tasks;
- Loss of appetite or disinterest in food;
- Indifference to her baby or not feeling attached or bonded;
- Feeling overwhelmed by her situation and feeling that there is no hope of things getting better; and,
- Feeling like she is just going through the motions of her day without being able to feel happy or joyful about anything.

I have known some women to experience some of these feelings. Many women are reluctant to tell *anyone* when they feel this way, because many people/women do not understand postpartum depression. It is a medical condition that requires attention and treatment.

Most postpartum depression is thought to be related to fluctuating hormone levels that affect mood and energy. Levels of estrogen and progesterone that increased during pregnancy drop suddenly after delivery. In some cases, a woman's thyroid hormone may decrease as well. These rapid hormone shifts affect the brain's mood chemistry in a way that can lead to sadness, low mood, and depression that lingers. Stress hormones may have an added effect on mood. Some women might experience this more than others.

If your feelings of sadness or depression are strong, if they linger throughout most of the day (for days at a time), or if they last longer than a week or two, then experts advise that you should talk to your doctor. A new mother who feels like giving up, who feels as though life is not worth living, or who has suicidal thoughts or feelings needs to tell her doctor right away. And I do not discount this at all.

### Brooke Shields

Do you remember the story about the actress Brooke Shields? She had it all: a happy marriage, celebrated beauty, world fame…yet, after her child was born, she fought the "mother-load" of emotional battles: a crippling bout with postpartum depression. After giving birth, Brooke Shields, while having received rave reviews on Broadway, suddenly found herself staring out of the window of her fourth-floor Manhattan apartment, contemplating putting an end to it all.

"I really didn't want to live anymore," she admitted frankly in an interview with WebMed.com. She said that, during this time, simply seeing a window was enough to prompt her to think, "I just want to leap out of my life." The rational side then took over and told her that she was only on the fourth floor and would get broken and life would be even worse. For Shields, the painful struggle to get pregnant and the ensuing slide into postpartum depression after her labor and delivery marked the most tumultuous time in her life.

The point is that postpartum depression can last for several months or even longer—if left untreated. With proper treatment, a woman can feel like herself again. Treatment may include talk therapy, medication, or both. In addition, proper diet, exercise, rest, and social support can be very helpful. Some research suggests that expressing thoughts and emotions through certain writing techniques can help relieve symptoms of depression.

If you are a new mom, then I know you understand all of this. It may take several weeks for a woman to begin to feel better once she is being treated for depression—though some begin to feel better sooner.

Take time for yourself! You cannot be a good mother to others unless you are a good mother to yourself. I have learned that as a mother in particular, it is easy to lose yourself in other things that appear more pressing. Women simply forget to take care of themselves because we are so busy taking care of "my child, my business, my clients…my family." You can and you must make yourself the priority. If you are healthy, then you can take better care of your loved ones. But to be able to do so, you must put yourself first.

To me, being a mother means making sure that my children are well looked after and protected. It means making sure they grow up to be responsible adults and compassionate human beings. In the early years, being a good mother meant surviving on as little as four or five hours of sleep a day. It also meant not being able to take time for *you*.

Just remember that the day will come when your kids are going to be teenagers who no longer want to hang out with their mom. You will be able to sleep in, take your showers in peace, have a meal without being interrupted, and have plenty of time for yourself; however, there will be other things to adjust to.

My being a mother does not mean giving up who I am as an individual; instead, it has added another dimension to my life. I am not just a mother—I am also an independent, professional, perfectly capable woman. As a role model to my daughter (and my son as well), I think it is important for them to see that their mom has her own interests, has her own hobbies, and needs time on her own as well.

I grew up with three sisters and I was the third sister. I often felt caught in the middle. So, I see life from both sides. I understand the older siblings *and* the younger siblings as well. With that being said, I have tried to be fair with my children and to establish a level playing ground when it comes to giving them the things they need—especially attention.

There is no doubt in my mind that one's relationship with his/her siblings affects the way he/she acts as a parent. All the feelings of love, admiration, jealousy, anger, and resentment that the parent felt toward his/her siblings—connected to his/her birth-order position—are projected onto his/her children and affect tremendously how he/she interacts with them.

If you are a firstborn child, then your parent(s) probably pressured you to achieve or to always do your best. Your having experienced this will affect the kinds of demands that you make on your own children. If you are a second-born child who was constantly criticized by his older sibling, then your having experienced this will govern how you—as a parent—interact with your children. Your birth-order experiences powerfully impact the parent-child relationship you have with your own children.

It is natural for a parent to perhaps unconsciously identify with a child of the same birth-order position…because that child reminds her/him of herself/himself. She/he may either feel affectionate toward a child from another birth-order position, or battle hard with him/her because of old unresolved feelings of jealousy and anger toward a sibling.

When reflecting on my children and how they were treated, I was very comfortable in the fairness that both received as young children; however, my daughter tells a different story. As a young woman today, she will not hesitate to tell me that Jim (her older brother) was favored and was treated better than she was. She will also tell me that he was listened to when she was not. She obviously did not feel as valued when comparing herself to her brother. Those were her feelings as a child and those feelings have not changed. She is still affected by what happened years ago. As a parent, I had no idea that those feelings will always be with her—and there is little I can do to change it. While talking to other family members and friends in gathering information for this book, I was amazed at the deep-rooted feelings that exist between family members which stem from the way they were treated because of their birth order. Birth order matters more than we realize.

Mixed feelings are a natural part of every relationship—even as a mother. As mothers, we can begin to look at how we react to each child. We know that all children are different and many times the child will see the differences that we make in communicating with the others. They will see our actions in a different light—one that we do not see ourselves. We tend to react based on our own past experiences as children, with little regard to how it affects our children.

When a mother, who is a second-born sibling, sees her daughter tease her younger sister the way the mother's older brother teased her, that mother will go right back to that child place. She becomes the baby who is being picked on and will often react out of a place of instinct.

A parent can strongly identify with the child who holds the same birth-order position as she/he does. If the child is the same sex or has the same temperament as the parent, then this identification will undoubtedly be more intense.

If a mother is a firstborn daughter with a second-born brother, and she has a firstborn daughter and a second-born son—thus, mirroring her own childhood and sibling relationship—then she will share a more kindred spirit between herself and her daughter. She can easily get frustrated about the actions of the younger brother because she relates to the situation; she has "been there, done that."

Parents generally do not recognize this tendency in the mother-child relationship or the father-child relationship. But parents are simply reenacting their own childhoods and birth-order relationships.

A strong parental identification can affect a child very positively (of course). The parent may be more sensitive to the child's issues. When parents experience their own early childhood pain in some way, they can use their deeper understanding to extend extra support to the child and assist him/her in working through his/her problems. But sometimes a parent can have a negative identification with his/her child. If the parent sees what appears to be an aspect of himself/herself in his/her child that he/she does not like, then he/she may get angry and behave negatively.

Fear and guilt are often the triggers of parental anger. I have honestly tried not to let it interfere in my role as a mother. One woman named Sarah said, "Whenever I see my older daughter hurting her younger brother, I see her as a reflection of myself. I feel guilty about the way I mistreated my younger sibling and I start screaming." One second-born father becomes enraged with his second-born son every time he gives up when he is trying something new. Realizing the source of his anger, he admitted this: "I often felt inadequate in relation to my older brother and would stop trying. I didn't want my son to be a quitter, too."

Most parents consciously or unconsciously set out to repair what happened to them in their families of origin. As parents, they try to correct all the wrongs that were done to them as children. In other words, if a mother has grown up with an abusive older brother, then that mother will not allow her own sons to say mean things to her youngest daughter. She will listen and watch and protect her. As the parent intervenes to create a more positive experience for his/her children, he/she can undergo an internal reparative process as well. If he/she helps the youngest child assert himself with an older sibling—something he/she could never do—then he/she will feel stronger and may be able to use the same skill with others. For example, if I intervene in a sibling battle to prevent my children from hurting each other, then I am fulfilling an unresolved wish that my own parents had stepped in to protect me. I also experience a vicarious pleasure, too, as I help my children to achieve a kind, loving relationship that is closer to the ideal sibling relationship that I always dreamed of.

I have friends who were "an only child." I have noticed that some of them will go to great lengths to have a second child because they do not want their child to feel the loneliness that they felt as an only child. However, perhaps a woman who was a younger sibling and who felt as though the older sibling was preferred might decide to have only one child (or no children at all), because she wants to reap the benefits of being the center of attention—or because she does not wish to relive the pain of her own sibling relationship via her children.

Unless you are a single mother (or father), there are generally two parents simultaneously playing out with their children their unresolved jealousy, anger, and resentment from their own sibling relationships. No wonder there is so much chaos in families! Sometimes, the two parents may come from the same birth-order position and act in concert. If they are both firstborns, for example, then they may each identify with their older child and support him/her when he/she fails at something; however, it is also possible that both parents may come down hard on him or her because they expect their first child to be "perfect."

In my observing my grandchildren, it is evident that there are differences in the way their parents react to them. Even though they are twins, the parents tend to have a better feel for what is going on with their daughter—who is the firstborn. Both parents are firstborns, which could be the reason why they may be more in tune with what is going on with their daughter. Many times we as parents tend to be unaware of the struggle that the second and/or younger child has in trying to be heard. I mentioned earlier that my daughter has reminded me often that her voice was not heard and that she did not receive the attention that her older brother received. We can do a better job when we are aware of the feelings of siblings (as they relate to birth order).

To ensure that you are a good mother, you must analyze your motives, intentions, and actions. We have already established that the parent's birth-order experience influences the parent-child relationship; hence, it is crucial that you try to be aware of your emotions and motives. It will help if you can connect your feelings to a real-life experience from the past. If you can do this, then you will feel tremendous relief.

For example, what if you feel jealous of your daughter because your husband is reading her a story? What if this reminds you of your older sister who received more attention from your mother than you did? If you identify this in yourself, then you will be far more forgiving of your emotion. You are not a bad mother. Your feeling stems from a real experience that you had in the past. When difficult feelings arise, it would be extremely helpful for you to identify personal experiences that are driving these emotions. Recalling the way you felt as a child will help you understand your feelings *now*.

As a middle child, I have often become the diplomat as the mother, as a sister, and as a friend. The negative side of this is that I do not like to make waves and will avoid conflict. This means that all kinds of storms can brew underneath because I am not communicating with my children the way I should. As a daughter, I tried to please my parents by taking over a lot of the care of my younger sister.

On the other hand, my husband creates a different scenario. He was the third-born, with two older sisters. It is more difficult to put him in a neat little package. Males with "all sisters" and no brothers create a different story. I have been the easy and protective parent, and he has been the more rigid parent.

---

*My dirty secret was this: I just didn't see what was so great about motherhood. My days felt like a marathon disaster movie, starring me racing around after my toddler to prevent him from hurling himself from high places. My nights were a study in sleep deprivation, with my daughter waking up every two hours and screaming from acid reflux.*

~Anonymous Online Blogger~

---

## *The Joy of Motherhood*

A couple of years ago, Oprah featured moms on her show. The two so-called "experts" who wrote the book were smart, business-type women who looked like they belonged on Wall Street instead of in a kitchen with children and spilled milk. These "experts" rallied the audience into a frenzy of confessions about motherhood and the hardships of this occupation.

"I hate the fluids of babies: pee, spit-up, spilt milk, snot."

"I cried the day I drove to the car dealership to buy a mini-van."

"There were days I wanted to send them back from whence they came."

There was a continuous flood of complaints from the audience of parents. Video clips of small kids on bikes, disastrous laundry rooms (cluttered with clothes and debris) were shown—all things to make one wonder why in the world anyone would want to have children. What I noticed most profoundly about the show was the "lack of joy" from these mothers. Everyone was acting like a victim…a "martyr." Oprah, never having mothered anyone, had to declare that indeed, they were right. Motherhood equaled sainthood, which makes us think of burning at the stake while saying, "It's all for being a good mom."

Sure, being a mother is difficult. As I have explained in earlier parts of this chapter, your birth order and your husband's birth order will affect the way you treat your own children and their birth order. But, overall, motherhood has been one of the happiest, most satisfying, life-giving, joyful, and rewarding experiences—jobs—I have ever had.

Being a mother is not a burden. My sense of who I am, my identity as a human being, and my self-knowledge have grown more through mothering than any job I have had, any degree I have earned, and any relationship I have pursued. I cannot think of anything that I would not do for my children.

The one crucial thing that these women in Oprah's audience forgot that day is unconditional love. When your baby is placed in your arms after it is born, your child loves you unconditionally. That love is overwhelming, infinite, and nonjudgmental. There is no greater love than God's love. Think about it: there is nothing more divine than a baby who falls asleep on your chest while you fall asleep. The whole world stops in this moment and you and the child fuse together as one. No meditation, prayer, yoga, prayer circle, or private retreat has ever come close to providing this depth of peace and love that a sleeping baby has given me. Those memories of my children as babies are songs in my heart.

Sure, as your children grow up, they will disappoint you and argue with you. They might tell you that they hate you and never want to see you again—but it is not real. The rewards for being a mother outweigh any of its challenges. And I, for one, consider being a mother a privilege. I am honored to be the mother of my children.

---

*"I had to do so much! I had never realized how hard it was to be everything for such a tiny creature. It was very demanding and at first I felt under-prepared and useless. Then she started being able to respond and I felt that the hard work and long days were really worth it."*

~Anonymous Online Blogger

---

*We seem to be doing a lot of parenting and not much else lately, which is as it should be. Every day we talk about how grateful we are for the good kids we have, and we go to bed tired because raising good kids takes a lot of effort and paper towels. And these days, a good Internet connection. How did I ever learn the states and their capitals without YouTube?*

~Anonymous Online Blogger

# Chapter Seven

# What It Means to Be a Friend

*"In everyone's life, at some time, our inner fire goes out. It is then burst into flame by an encounter with another human being. We should all be thankful for those people who rekindle the inner spirit."*
~Albert Schweitzer

**In this chapter, we will take a look at what it means to be a friend.** The contents of this chapter actually touch on every other chapter in this book. In writing about *My Mother, My Daughter, My Sister, My Friend*, I would be negligent if I did not address the "friend" aspect of our relationships with others. I consider myself a friend to my mother, to my daughter, to my son, and to my sisters and brothers. We may have started as family members, but we have ended up as friends—imperfections and all. If we are good friends to our *daughters*, our *mothers*, our *sons,* our *husbands*, and our *families*, then we will be good friends to other people in our lives. If we practice deception, manipulation, and dishonesty with our family members, then these things will become a part of our relationships with others.

None of us started out as friends. As a mother, I have had to be a *mother* first, and a friend second. Webster defines a friend as a person whom one knows well and is fond of, an intimate associate, a close acquaintance, and a person on the same side in a struggle. Friendship develops as we get to know each other and begin to enjoy some of the same things.

There are times when parents treat their children as friends. If you have a tendency to treat your child as a "friend," you should understand the meaning of friendship: Friends are a group of people that has the same notion about ideas and life. The truth is that children and adults have very different ideas about their approach to life. They have entirely different ideas about what is right and what is wrong. They have very different ideas about decision making. Being a caring, responsible parent comes first. As the child matures, your friendship with him/her develops. Know that there is a difference between parenting and friendship.

For children, friendship is influenced by family experiences. A variety of studies suggests that children who have a secure attachment to their parents have a better-quality friendship. Studies of young children have found that popularity in preschool is linked with verbal ability, kindness, and low aggression.

With infants, when a mother or father demonstrates his or her love by holding, talking to, and singing to the child, a special bond is created. This bond can be the key to helping the child develop friendships in the future. If the child feels secure as a child growing up, he/she will feel more secure as an adult. If a child is uncomfortable, tense, and/or insecure as a child, then he/she will have problems developing friendships while progressing into adulthood.

As a child grows older, the parent finds him-/herself in a different role and sometimes finds him-/herself less emotional (not as loving) when it comes to the child. This can become difficult for parents who want to be their child's "best friend."

Can a parent be a child's best friend? A recent study revealed that 43 percent of today's parents are seeking acceptance and friendship from their teens. Forty percent of these parents said that they wanted to accomplish their primary objective: to be their child's best friend. It is evident that when you become your child's best friend, you give up your position of authority. Can you be effective as a parent if you have given your authority to your child?

I think parents often make the mistake of making their child their friend/confidante. So when they say, "I want to be his friend, and I want him to be my friend," what they are really saying is, "I want to be able to confide in him/her." That just does not fit with the functional role of a parent, or the decision-making role of the parent.

It is a very well-meaning trap that parents can fall into. If parents begin to discuss personal issues with the child, this sharing can be ineffective for the child—because the child is not morally, emotionally, or intellectually prepared to play the role of confidante. If you are forty years old and you want a confidante, find someone closer to your age. It is not fair to the child. Children are not emotionally mature enough to make sound decisions about the problems of others.

When you make your child your confidante, you are saying that you and the child are co-decision makers. You are treating the child like one of your peers. But the fact is that you and your child are not and should not be co-decision makers. It is not fair to have children make decisions that adults should make.

However, you can certainly be straight with a child without putting undo pressure on him/her. One of the things you can share with a child is the statement, "We can't afford that." It is a factual statement that explains the limits under which you must live. Statements such as "I don't know how I'm going to pay the rent this month" are topics/subjects that the child is not prepared for, which will develop in him/her a way of looking at the world that is unhealthy and unrealistic. Those kinds of statements can be very stressful for a child or teen.

Many parents try to raise their children in a way that mirrors how they wish their parents had parented them. It has been said that we parent the way that we were parented. So just because your parents may have been distant or rigid with you, seemed uncaring or self-involved to you, or made horrible personal mistakes and did not give you the guidance you felt that you needed does not mean that you should overcompensate for that by letting the child cross boundaries in an unsafe or insensible way. However, once the child is a grown adult and is out working on his/her own and paying his/her own way in the world, then you can be more of a friend to your child.

When we are interacting with our children, we must remember that anything done in a reactionary way is going to have unforeseen consequences. The biggest problem with parent-child friendships lies in all the unforeseen consequences. Parents tend to look only at the foreseen consequences—failing to realize that our children have thoughts and feelings and they also know what they like and what they dislike. Their thoughts will not always be in line with our thoughts; and there will come a time when they will challenge us and our way of thinking.

Many parents feel abandoned by their child when they have parented too much, not giving the child an opportunity to make decisions that they are capable of making. They feel a sense of loss when the child does not comply with their wants, and they compensate for it by blaming the child.

In his book, *The Mother Factor: How Your Mother's Emotional Legacy Impacts Your Life*, Dr. Stephan Poulter (U.S. family psychologist) writes, "When mothers become best friends to their children, it leaves their children motherless." Being a strong parent can be uncomfortable for some of us. One friend said she hated getting cross with her children when she got home from work because that was their only time together and she did not want to spoil it by chastising them. On another occasion, a friend said that she was going to punish her daughter's bad behavior by saying that she would not take her out to lunch and shopping—but then realized that her enforcing this punishment would mean that she herself could not go; so she gave in and the daughter never received any repercussions for her bad behavior.

Wanting to be a friend to your child can be disastrous. No one wants a return to the idea of Victorian parenting (with its overtones of children being seen and not heard), but we *do* need to reestablish a sense of parental authority. Feeling they have a friend instead of a mother can lead to confusion and create insecurities as well. There is also research that indicates that boys whose mothers do not stand up to them, especially if they are single mothers with no male influence in the household, can be disruptive in schools, as well as dismissive of women.

Of course, it is healthy for parents to get along with their children—to chat and laugh together—but it is not healthy for mothers to insist that their daughters "tell them everything." I did not tell my mother "everything," and have never expected my own children to do that, either. Daughters who have been brought up with a clear sense that they have a mother instead of an aging best friend will not need or want their mother to act like their best friend.

### A Mother's Role as Friend

Yes, it is true. A mother has a multitude of roles; however, being your daughter's best friend is not one of them. If your daughter views you as her friend, then she will be more likely to come to you with problems and ask questions when faced with difficult decisions about drinking, drugs, sex, and life. However, you should be aware that you might learn some things that will be uncomfortable for both of you.

On the flipside, a mother's being close to her daughter can be very beneficial throughout her teenage years, because she can talk to her daughter and keep her from making many mistakes that are avoidable. A mother may also discourage her teenager from having certain friends, taking certain risks, and experiencing new things. In other words, the mother may think that she can be the "everything" to her child—but she cannot.

In order to grow into adults, your children must develop confidence, independence, and responsibility, and they must make some mistakes on their own and suffer the consequences. If a mother is too much of a friend, then a teenager may not have the opportunity to experience such growth.

Coming from a large family with six brothers and three sisters gave me a reason to feel guilty that my children did not experience the variety of interactions that I had experienced as a child. I wanted to be a friend to my children; however, there were many times when the friendship ended and the parenting began.

You must continue to provide your children with structure, discipline, and stability until they reach adulthood. And though there may be many disagreements and challenges along the way, balancing the roles of mother and friend to your children will help them develop into healthy, happy, and productive adults. Once your child becomes that healthy, happy adult, you can then let your relationship transition into more of a friendship.

### *What It Means to Be a Friend to Other Women*

*"Good friends are like stars. You don't always see them but you know they're always there!"*
~Author Unknown

After years of being a counselor in school and speaking with other women on the topic of friendship, I have discovered a pattern of characteristics that women typically appreciate in other people. I encourage you to consider the following qualities in light of your current friendships and, if you are married, in light of your relationship with your spouse. These are qualities to internalize in your own life in order to become a better friend. You can also use them as a measure to consider potential friendships in the future.

Here are the top seven relationship ingredients that have surfaced over the years…

***Take a Genuine Interest in Others…*** On Simon & Schuster's Web site *Tips on Life & Love*, in the article, "The 7 Qualities of a Good Friend," Dale Carnegie, author of *How to Win Friends and Influence People*, says this:

> "You can make more friends in two months by becoming interested in other people than you can in two years by trying to get people interested in you." As we listen to others and show an interest in what is important to them, we begin to truly love and understand them. Every person has an invisible sign around his or her neck that reads, "I want to feel important." Everyone has something to offer this world. We need to search for it, find it, and bring it to the surface.

Scheduling time for others is a good way to make time to be attentive to others. What does this mean? It means that you set aside a certain amount of time that you devote 100 percent to someone else. Perhaps you can devote an hour per week, or maybe longer.

Everyone is so busy these days that it is not silly to think of scheduling a time to be there for someone. You write this down on a schedule and then, when you meet that person for coffee or a phone call, you focus solely on your friend and his/her needs. I know that for me, if something is not on the calendar, then it typically does not happen. A "scheduled appointment" for personal time with a friend is a time when we can write a note or make a call or deliver a gift or do a favor; it is a time when we can even pray for a certain friend in need.

***Be a Giver, Not a Taker…*** Ask not what your friends can give to you, but, rather, what you can give to your friends. (Sound familiar? That is a version of President John F. Kennedy's motto.) *What can we give to others?* How about a smile, a hug, a kind word, a listening ear, a prayer, an encouraging note, a meal, or help with an errand? We can come up with many things to give others—if we are willing to be attentive to their needs. Naturally, you must know someone's needs by taking a genuine interest in the person first. If you do not know that person's needs, then you are not being a good friend.

Giving may take time. It may take us out of our way. But giving and self-sacrifice help comprise the definition of love. Here is a sweet poem by John Oxenham:

> Art thou lonely, O my brother?
> Share thy little with another!
> Stretch a hand to one unfriended,
> And thy loneliness is ended.

***Be Loyal...*** Loyalty is a rare commodity in today's world, but it is an absolute requirement in true and abiding friendships. When we are loyal to one friend, we prove ourselves worthy of many. If we are disloyal to one friend, then we will find that we are disloyal to others.

One way that we can show our loyalty is through our words—or lack thereof. In fact, a key to being loyal is keeping a tight rein on our tongues. If we are loyal, then we will not tear a friend down behind her back or share her personal story without her permission. It is easy to gossip or pass judgment; it is much harder to keep silent.

Marsha Sinetar, who became famous with her best-selling book, *Do What You Love, The Money Will Follow: Discovering Your Right Livelihood,* once said this: "When you find yourself judging someone, silently say to yourself, 'They are doing the best they can right now.' Then mentally forgive yourself for judging." Hence, as positive women, we need to make sure our tongues are used for good and not evil. We should be builders with our words, not demolishers. Jealousy, envy, and a range of other negative emotions can keep us from being loyal. But true loyalty overcomes all of them.

There was a beautiful *Old Testament* story about the friendship between Jonathan and David. Jonathan had reason to be jealous of his friend, David. Jonathan was King Saul's son and in line to succeed his father to the throne—but God anointed David to be the next king, instead. At the same time, David easily could have been angry with Jonathan. Jonathan's father, the king, chased David out of the country and tried to kill him. Yet, these two men pledged their loyalty in friendship and never wavered in their decision. Eventually, Jonathan saved David's life, and David continued to show his loyalty to his friend by watching out for Jonathan's son.

Jealousy, envy, bitterness, and anger are all sisters in sin and killers of loyalty in relationships. But if we continually take these emotions to God and ask for His help in overcoming them, then we can remain loyal to our friends through the thick and thin of life.

***Be a Positive Person...*** The most consistent comment I hear about what people want in friendships is this: "I want a friend I can laugh with." We all want friends we can enjoy! People who consistently bring us down with their problems and complaints are generally not the ones we want to pal around with for any length of time. Of course, sometimes a friend will go through a difficult time, at which time we need to be ready and willing to hold a hand and provide a listening ear.

But a friend in need is different from a habitual whiner. We want our friendships to be positive and uplifting—and that means that we must be positive, uplifting friends ourselves.

It has been said that there are two kinds of people: those who brighten the room when they enter, and those who brighten the room when they leave. Let us make sure that we are brightening our friendships with our presence. Positive women demonstrate attitudes and spirits that see God at work in all of life, and they encourage others to see Him as well. They are generous with praise, with smiles, and with love. In the same vein, Francis Bacon—English philosopher, statesman, scientist, jurist, and author (1561-1626)—said this: "Friendship doubles joys and halves grief."

***Appreciate the Differences in Others...*** Variety is the spice of life. I am so glad that when I walk into an ice cream store, vanilla is not the only option! At the same token, I am also glad that God created people with a variety of personalities, talents, ethnicities, and interests. And this is the case because each one of us is a unique creation.

So why is it that instead of appreciating our differences, we tend to despise them or become jealous of them? It is because along with a variety of personalities comes a variety of faults. With that in mind, we must always remember that none of us is perfect—and that no one should judge another. (I will write more about the differences in others in the next chapter, but the topic was worth mentioning in this one concerning friendship.)

***Build on Common Interests...*** What is it that brings friends together in the first place? There is usually something that draws us to others: a common hobby, a common background, a sport, a religious or Bible study group, a volunteer project, or perhaps a children's activity. Some of your friendships may develop through taking your kids to school and to mutual activities. Some develop through church affiliations, which create a common bond.

In our busy society, it can be difficult to create times to get together with people. But if we take advantage of the common activities and interests we have with others, then we can fit the time for friendship into our schedules. If you and a friend both like to exercise, then work out together. If you both like to read, then go to the bookstore together to pick out your next selection, grab some coffee, and talk about the last book you read. If your kids are your common interest, then consider getting together on a regular basis to pray for them. The point is to allow your common interests to draw you together.

Married couples need to practice this, too. Many couples tend to get focused on (and frustrated with) their differences while overlooking the common interests that brought them together in the first place. When that happens, they need to get back to basics and begin to build again on their common interests—overlooking each other's faults and appreciating the different qualities they bring to the marriage.

Marriages seem to be made in heaven when they start, but they most assuredly need to be maintained and continually tended here on Earth. Mignon McLaughlin, author of *The Complete Neurotic's Notebook,* puts it this way: "A successful marriage requires falling in love many times, always with the same person."

***Be Open, Honest, and Real…*** The word *hypocrite* originally described actors on a stage who covered their faces with masks in order to conceal their real identities. Today, the word describes people who pretend to be something that they are not.

True friendship cannot be built on false images. We must be true to ourselves. We may think that we have to present a faultless picture of ourselves to the rest of the world…but why? No one wants to be friends with someone who is perfect! We simply need to be our best selves and allow people to know the real us.

Of course, being open and honest does not equate to our spilling our guts to everyone. We must discern between those casual friendships and those deep friendships which we can trust with our hearts. As we already know, loyalty is a rare commodity; when we find it, we know we have a friend we can trust—someone with whom we can share openly about our deepest issues and feelings. George Washington offered some wise words about friendship when he said, "Be courteous to all, but intimate with few; and let those few be well tried before you give them your confidence. True friendship is a plant of slow growth and must undergo and withstand the shocks of adversity before it is entitled to the appellation."

As for being a friend to your child, remember that you will be a parent *first*. When your child grows into adulthood, then you can transition to friend mode.

### A Final Note about Being Friends with Your Daughters—Your Children

Clearly, parental involvement continues in the life of the grownup child and there are ample opportunities for disagreements, debates, or even serious conflicts while trying to live together. But the ultimate aim should be to coexist in harmony—in a relationship of mutual respect—without dependence or domination by either on the other. It is important to accept differences and leave enough space for respectful negotiation.

When it comes to protecting, being assertive with, and sheltering a child, achieving the correct balance is necessary. Being overprotective can be as much of a problem as allowing too much freedom. Parents need to teach responsibility and help the child understand that there will come a time when he/she will be responsible for taking care of himself/herself.

Preparing the child for the future is important. Good parenting of a grownup child requires the acknowledgment that the child is now an adult and is capable of exercising what he/she has been taught by his/her parent(s).

There can be conflict when the child's views, opinions, and choices are different from those of her/his parents'. The process ends with both parent and child respecting each other's attitudes and behaviors.

Good parenting requires one to provide the comfort and support to the child or adult when needed; however, there comes a point in every parent's life when he/she has to learn to "let go" and realize that everybody has to go through the growing-up experience alone. The parent must give the child enough space and strength and put enough faith in the child's potential to work out her/his problems on her/his own. Doing this gives the child an opportunity to *know* that he/she can work out his/her own problems.

When you are comfortable in the knowledge that you have helped your child grow to be a responsible individual who can make responsible decisions and can take care of him-/herself and others (if necessary), that is a very rewarding feeling.

*"Some people need a red carpet rolled out in front of them in order to walk forward into friendship. They can't see the tiny, outstretched hands all around them, everywhere, like leaves on trees."*

~Miranda July

---

*"Your friend is your needs answered.*

*He is your field which you sow with love and reap with thanksgiving.*

*And he is your board and your fireside.*

*For you come to him with your hunger, and you seek him for peace."*

~On Friendship, Kahlil Gibran

# *Chapter Eight*

# What It Means to Be a Woman: Empowering Women Everywhere

*"The more you praise and celebrate your life,
the more there is in life to celebrate."*
~Oprah Winfrey

*"Where there is no struggle, there is no strength."*
~Oprah Winfrey

We women are a force to be reckoned with these days. We feel that we are no longer limited by the profession that we choose. We no longer sit back and expect a man to take care of us. We are more confident when

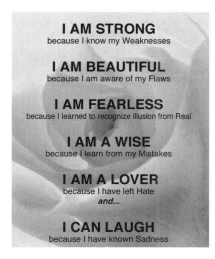

**I AM STRONG**
because I know my Weaknesses

**I AM BEAUTIFUL**
because I am aware of my Flaws

**I AM FEARLESS**
because I learned to recognize illusion from Real

**I AM A WISE**
because I learn from my Mistakes

**I AM A LOVER**
because I have left Hate
*and...*

**I CAN LAUGH**
because I have known Sadness

we make our choices. We women are out making a difference; we hold positions that were not ours to hold ten to fifteen years ago; we go to college; we become doctors, lawyers, teachers, and entrepreneurs; and, most importantly, we are mothers, and we are daughters, sisters, and friends. I want to take this time to devote a section of this book to women who helped blaze trails for all of us. I, for one, am so grateful for those who have paved the way and have helped us to know that we can do whatever we want to do.

### *Susan Brownell Anthony*

Many women in history have been instrumental in the progress that women have made in their careers, positions, and jobs that are not thought to be fit for women to execute. Susan Brownwell Anthony may be classified as a feminist who preached women's rights. Susan was born February 15, 1820, in Adams, Massachusetts. She was a prominent American civil rights leader who played a pivotal role in the nineteenth-century women's rights movement to introduce women's suffrage to the United States. She also co-founded the women's rights journal, *The Revolution*. She traveled the United States and Europe, and averaged seventy-five to one hundred speeches per year. She has been touted as one of the important advocates in leading the way for women's rights to be acknowledged and instituted in the American government.

Anthony fought to abolish slavery and for the right for women to own their own property and retain their earnings. In 1900, Anthony persuaded the University of Rochester to admit women.

Anthony, who remained single, had much compassion for the cause of women. She had a keen mind and the ability to inspire others. She remained active until her death on March 13, 1906. Her attributes are an example for all of us to follow.

### *Rosa Louise McCauley Parks*

Many of us remember Rosa Louise McCauley Parks, an African-American civil rights activist whom the U.S. Congress called "the First Lady of Civil Rights," and "The mother of the freedom movement."

On December 1, 1955, in Montgomery, Alabama, Parks made history when she refused to obey bus driver James F. Blake's order that she give up her seat to make room for a white passenger. Park's civil disobedience had the effect of sparking the Montgomery Bus Boycott. Her act of defiance became an important symbol of the modern Civil Rights Movement—and Parks became an international icon of resistance to racial segregation. She organized and collaborated with civil rights leader Rev. Martin Luther King Jr., helping to launch him to national prominence in the Civil Rights Movement.

Parks received many honors ranging from the 1979 Spingarn Medal to the Presidential Medal of Freedom, the Congressional Gold Medal, and a posthumous statue in the United States Capitol's National Statuary Hall. Rosa Parks was the first woman and second non-U.S. government official granted the posthumous honor of lying in honor at the Capitol Rotunda.

Over the years, many brave women have played a very important role in establishing rights for all of us women. There are many additional women whose voices were defining factors in the role that women play today. The courage shown by Rosa Parks is to be admired, and the courage that she had is the courage that all of us can learn from. Remember that you have the courage to do more than you have dreamed. You have the courage to make the changes in your life that you have probably "dreamed about." Always look ahead. For the ladies in this chapter, it probably took one thought for them to make changes that affected all of us.

---

*"All changes start with one idea.*
*Changes are made when actions follow that idea."*
~Chris Norris

---

### Margaret Higgins Sanger

Another remarkable woman who has helped women achieve independence is Margaret Higgins Sanger. Sanger was an American sex educator, nurse, and birth control activist. Sanger opened the first birth-control clinic in the United States, and established *Planned Parenthood.* Whether or not you believe in birth control is not important; what is important is the way Sanger fought for women's rights.

In her early years, Sanger was a social activist in New York. Her actions were prompted by the suffering she witnessed due to frequent pregnancies and self-induced abortions. Sanger's mother endured eighteen pregnancies in twenty-two years, and died at the age of fifty from tuberculosis and cervical cancer. She developed an interest in women and birth control at an early age.

In 1916, Sanger opened the first birth-control clinic in the United States. She was arrested for distributing information on contraception. Her subsequent trial and appeal generated enormous support for her cause. Sanger felt that women needed to be able to determine when to bear children. She also wanted to prevent back-alley abortions, which were not only dangerous, but also illegal.

In 1912, Sanger founded the American Birth Control League, which later became the Planned Parenthood Federation of America. Sanger founded the first birth-control clinic staffed by an all-female doctor roster. She also started a birth-control clinic in Harlem—run by an entirely African-American staff.

From 1952 to 1959, Sanger served as president of the International Planned Parenthood Federation. She died in 1966, and is widely regarded as a founder of the modern birth-control movement. As you have read, Sanger has played a pivotal role in making changes for women and making it possible for women to make decisions that were not possible for them to make in the not-too-distant past. We applaud Sanger for her work and her interest to make changes that affect many mothers, daughters, sisters, and friends.

### Dr. Maya Angelou

Dr. Maya Angelou is one of the most influential voices of our time. Dr. Angelou is a celebrated poet, memoirist, novelist, educator, dramatist, producer, actress, historian, filmmaker, and civil rights activist.

She was born on April 4, 1928, in St. Louis, Missouri. Dr. Angelou was raised in St. Louis and Stamps, Arkansas. In Stamps, Dr. Angelou experienced the brutality of racial discrimination. She had a strong faith and the values of the traditional African-American family, community, and culture.

Dr. Angelou has accomplished many things: I will name some of those to give you an idea of what she has done and what you can do as a powerful woman—a mother, a daughter, a sister, a friend: Dr. Angelou toured Europe with a production of the opera *Porgy and Bess*. She studied modern dance with Martha Graham, and dance with Alvin Ailey on television variety shows; she acted in the historic Off-Broadway production of Jean Genet's *The Blacks*, and wrote and performed *Cabaret for Freedom*; she taught at the University of Ghana's School of Music and Drama, and worked as feature editor for *The African Review*, and wrote for *The Ghanaian Times*; published in 1970, *I Know Why the Caged Bird Sings* was published to international acclaim and enormous popular success.

**A Strong Woman**
is one who feels deeply
and loves fiercely
Her tears flow just as abundantly
as her laughter...

**A Strong Woman**
is both soft and powerful
She is both practical and spiritual...

**A Strong Woman**
in her essence
is a gift to the world...

Dr. Angelou has served on two presidential committees, was awarded the Presidential Medal of Arts in 2000 and the Lincoln Medal in 2008, and has received three Grammy awards. President Clinton requested that she compose a poem to read at his inauguration in 1993. Dr. Angelou's reading of her poem, "On the Pulse of the Morning," was broadcast live around the world.

Dr. Angelou has received over thirty honorary degrees and is a Reynolds Professor of American Studies at Wake Forest University. Her words and actions "stir our souls, energize our bodies, liberate our minds, and heal our hearts."

And while we cannot all be like Dr. Maya Angelou, we can strive to be the best we can be in our own lives.

### Oprah Winfrey

*(The book is by no means large enough to tell you about all of the accomplishments of Oprah Gail Winfrey; however, I will mention a few.)*

Oprah Gail Winfrey, known as "America's Beloved Best Friend," was born on January 29, 1954. She is loved and respected by many.

Born to an unwed teenage mother, Oprah spent her first years on her grandmother's farm in Kosciusko, Mississippi. Her grandmother taught her to read at the age of three, and she was reciting poems and Bible verses in churches. Life was not easy, but her grandmother gave her love and she was loved by her church community as well. They seemed to know that she had a gift.

At age 6, she was sent to Milwaukee to live with her mother, who worked as a housemaid. There were many days when her mother was not present to care for her. Oprah was repeatedly molested by male relatives and another visitor. The abuse lasted from the ages of nine to thirteen. When she tried to run away, she was sent to a juvenile detention home. She was unable to stay in the home because all the beds were filled. At age 14, she was out of the house and on her own. Oprah admitted to being sexually promiscuous as a teenager. After giving birth to a baby boy who died in infancy, she went to Nashville, Tennessee, to live with her father, Vernon Winfrey.

She was able to live in a home that was secure; however, her father, Vernon, was a strict disciplinarian. He required her to read a book and write a book report each week. He wanted her to have a good life, and "he would not accept anything less than what he thought was the best."

In this structured environment, Oprah did well: she became an honor student, winning prizes for oratory and dramatic recitation.

At age 17, Oprah Winfrey won the Miss Black Tennessee beauty pageant and was offered a job at the radio station WVOL. She also won a full scholarship to Tennessee State University, where she majored in Speech Communications and Performing Arts.

In 1976, she moved to Baltimore to join WJZ-TV News as a co-anchor—and she co-hosted her first talk show, *People Are Talking*.

In January of 1984, she was invited to Chicago to host a faltering half-hour morning program on WLS-TV. She immediately turned *AM Chicago* into the hottest show in town. The show was renamed *The Oprah Winfrey Show* in September of 1985.

A year later, *The Oprah Winfrey Show* was broadcast nationally, and became the number-one talk show in national syndication. Oprah's show won three Daytime Emmy Awards in the categories of "Outstanding Host," "Outstanding Talk/Service Program," and "Outstanding Director." The following year, the show received its second consecutive Emmy as "Outstanding Talk/Service Program." *(Oprah's awards are too numerous to name in this book.)*

By the time America fell in love with Oprah Winfrey—the talk-show host—she had already captured the nation's attention with her poignant portrayal of Sofia in Steven Spielberg's 1985 adaptation of Alice Walker's novel, *The Color Purple. The Color Purple* earned nominations for an Oscar and a Golden Globe Award as "Best Supporting Actress."

Oprah Winfrey has her own production company. She is a partner in Oxygen Media, Inc., a cable channel and interactive network presenting programming designed primarily for women, and most recently has her own television network—OWN—which is in its initial stages. She has also published two magazines: *O, The Oprah Magazine*, and *O at Home*. In 2000, Oprah's Angel Network began presenting a $100,000 "Use Your Life Award" to people who are using their own lives to improve the lives of others. When *Forbes* published its list of America's billionaires for the year 2003, it disclosed that Oprah Winfrey was the first African-American woman to become a billionaire.

Oprah Winfrey has been ranked the richest African American of the twentieth century and the greatest black philanthropist in American history—and was, for a time, the world's only black billionaire.

Words cannot tell you how Ms. Oprah Gail Winfrey has influenced my life. I can tell you that she has inspired and motivated me in ways that I cannot measure. I watched her first show and have been and continue to be motivated by her shows over the years. When Oprah announced that she was going to do her last show, my daughter and I went into panic mode. Oprah has most definitely influenced my life, my daughter's life, my sisters' lives, and my friends' lives as well. Thank you, Ms. Winfrey, for using your life to teach us, inspire us, motivate us, and help us understand the importance of community service and showing us that we can experience/"live our best life"—and we should be about the business of helping others.

### Barbara Walters

Barbara Walters was born September 25, 1929, in Boston, Massachusetts—the daughter of Dena Seletsky Walters and nightclub impresario, Lou Walters. She had two siblings: older sister Jacqueline, who was born developmentally disabled and died in 1985, and brother Burton, who died of pneumonia in 1932.

I cannot say enough about Barbara Walters. She has paved the way for so many women in journalism and other areas of television as well. She attended Sarah Lawrence College in Bronxville, New York, graduating in 1953 with a Bachelor's degree in English. Barbara landed her first job in journalism as the assistant to publicity director and Republican activist Tex McCary of WRCA-TV. This job provided Barbara with the opportunity to develop her writing and producing skills, enabling her to write material for the CBS network's *Morning Show*.

In 1961, Barbara Walters was hired to work as a researcher and writer for the popular *Today Show*. Her initial assignments were stories slanted toward female viewers.

Walters worked on the *Today Show*, alongside Hugh Downs and, later, Frank McGee, and earned the nickname, the "Today Girl." Though serving as a co-host on the show, she was not given that official billing until 1974.

Walters remained on the show for eleven years. She established herself as a competent journalist in 1972, and was chosen to be part of the press corps that accompanied President Nixon on his historic trip to China. In 1975, she won her first Daytime Entertainment Emmy Award for best host in a talk series.

Walters was given a one-million-dollar annual salary, which was unheard of at that time. She was chosen to moderate the third and final presidential debate between challenger Jimmy Carter and incumbent President Gerald Ford. She also introduced the first of a series of *Barbara Walters Specials* in 1976. Her first interview on her program featured President Jimmy Carter and First Lady Rosalynn Carter. After this interview, she was known for her probing interview style. Her skills in asking questions as well as her interview style were admired by many. She was also very determined to get the "first interview" from a wide range of people. Her ability to know how to ask the questions the public would most like to hear without alienating the people she interviewed contributed to her success as a journalist.

Over the years, Barbara Walters has refined the art of "personality journalism" and "being the first" interviews. Walters has conducted timely interviews with world leaders. They include the Shah of Iran, Mohammad Reza Pahlavi; the U.K.'s first woman prime minister, Margaret Thatcher; the Dalai Lama; Russia's first post-communist president, Boris Yeltsin; and Venezuelan President Hugo Chavez.

In August of 1997, Barbara Walters premiered a mid-morning talk show called *The View*, for which she is co-executive producer and co-host. The program features unique perspectives from five women on politics, family, careers, and general public-interest topics.

Some of the awards and honors received by Walters include the President's Award (in 1988); induction into the Academy of Television Arts & Sciences Hall of Fame in 1990; the Lowell Thomas Award for a career in journalism excellence in 1990; the Lifetime Achievement Award from the International Women's Media Foundation in 1991; the Muse Award from New York Women in Film and Television in 1997; the Lifetime Achievement Award from the National Academy of Television Arts and Sciences in 2000; and a star on the Hollywood Walk of Fame in 2007—as well as thirty-four daytime and primetime Emmy awards. Walters has also received honorary doctoral degrees from Ben-Gurion University in Jerusalem, Hofstra University, Marymount College, Ohio State University, Sarah Lawrence College, Temple University, and Wheaton College.

### First Lady Michelle Obama

According to *Biography.com*, Michelle LaVaughn Robinson Obama was born January 17, 1964, in Chicago, Illinois.

Michelle Obama was raised on Chicago's south side in a one-bedroom apartment. Her father, Frasier Robinson, was a city pump operator and a

Democratic precinct captain. Her mother, Marian, was a Spiegel's secretary who later stayed home to raise Michelle and her older brother, Craig. Michelle worked as a lawyer, a Chicago city administrator, and a community outreach worker, and is presently the wife of U.S. President Barack Obama.

Craig and Michelle, sixteen months apart in age, were often mistaken for twins. Both children were raised with an emphasis on education. By sixth grade, Michelle was attending gifted classes, where she learned French and took accelerated courses. She then went on to attend the city's first magnet high school for gifted children where, among other activities, she served as the student government treasurer.

After graduating from Whitney M. Young Magnet High School in Chicago's West Loop as class salutatorian, Michelle attended Princeton University, graduating cum laude in 1985 with a B.A. in Sociology. She went on to earn a J.D. from Harvard Law School in 1988.

Following law school, Michelle worked as an associate in the Chicago branch of the law firm Sidley Austin—in the area of marketing and intellectual property.

Michelle soon launched a career in public service, serving as an assistant to Mayor Daley and then as the assistant commissioner of planning and development for the City of Chicago. In 1993, she became Executive Director for the Chicago office of Public Allies, a non-profit leadership-training program that helped young adults develop skills for future careers in the public sector.

Michelle joined the University of Chicago in 1996 as associate dean of student services, developing the University's first community service program. She then worked for the University of Chicago Hospitals as executive director of community relations and external affairs.

She was appointed vice president of community relations and external affairs at the University of Chicago Medical Center, where she continues to work part-time. While managing the business diversity program, Michelle sat on six boards, including the prestigious Chicago Council on Global Affairs, and the University of Chicago Laboratory Schools.

Michelle Obama scaled back her own professional career to focus on family and Barack's campaign obligations during his run for the Democratic presidential nomination. Michelle says that she has made a "commitment to be away overnight only once a week—to campaign only two days a week and be home by the end of the second day" for their two daughters, Malia (born 1998) and Natasha "Sasha" (born 2001). Michelle's mother, Marian, played an important role in helping to take care of the girls while their parents campaign. "I've never participated at this level in any of his campaigns," Michelle says. "I have usually chosen to just appear when necessary." However, her husband's political role pushed the Obama family into the spotlight.

Michelle was featured in *Essence* magazine as one of "25 of the World's Most Inspiring Women," and in "The Harvard 100," a list of the most influential alumni for the year.

As the forty-fourth First Lady of the United States, Michelle Obama has focused much of her attention on issues such as the support of military families, helping working women balance career and family, and encouraging national service. Michelle volunteered at homeless shelters and soup kitchens in the Washington, D.C. area. She has also spoken out about the importance of public schools, and the importance of education and volunteer work.

Mrs. Obama has been very active in helping others understand the importance of diet and good health. In March of 2009, Michelle worked with twenty-three fifth graders from a local school in Washington, D.C., to plant a 1,100-square-foot garden of fresh vegetables and install beehives on the South Lawn of the White House. She has put efforts to fight childhood obesity near the top of her agenda.

Mrs. Michelle Obama is continuing to work for children and education. Mrs. Obama gives us hope and she is an inspiration to all of us.

### *Hillary Diane Rodham Clinton*

According to *Wikipedia*, Hillary Diane Rodham Clinton (born October 26, 1947) is the sixty-seventh United States Secretary of State, serving in the administration of President Barack Obama. She was a United States Senator for New York from 2001 to 2009. As the wife of the forty-second President of the United States, Bill Clinton, she was the First Lady of the United States from 1993 to 2001. In the 2008 election, Clinton was a leading candidate for the Democratic presidential nomination.

A native of Illinois, Hillary Rodham first attracted national attention in 1969 for her remarks as the first student commencement speaker at Wellesley College. She graduated from Yale Law School in 1973. She moved to Arkansas in 1974 and married Bill Clinton in 1975. Some of her achievements include (but are not limited to) the following: she co-founded the Arkansas Advocates for Children and Families in 1977; became the first female chair of the Legal Services Corporation in 1978; was named the first female partner at Rose Law Firm in 1979; was twice listed as one of the 100 most influential lawyers in America; and successfully led a task force to reform Arkansas's education system.

After moving to the state of New York, Clinton was elected as a U.S. Senator in 2000; that election marked the first time that an American First Lady had run for public office. Clinton was also the first female senator to represent the state.

Senator Clinton was reelected by a wide margin in 2006. In the 2008 presidential nomination race, Hillary Clinton won more primaries and delegates than any other female candidate in American history.

Upon her being appointed as Obama's Secretary of State, Clinton became the first former First Lady to serve in a President's Cabinet. She has been put at the forefront of the U.S. response to the Arab Spring, including advocating for the military intervention in Libya. She has used "smart power" as the strategy for asserting U.S. leadership and values in the world and has championed the use of social media in getting the U.S. message out.

Secretary of State Hillary Clinton was named the most popular person in the world. She was the first *First Lady* to hold a post-graduate degree, and to have her own professional career up to the time of entering the White House. She was also the first to have an office in the West Wing of the White House—in addition to the usual First Lady offices in the East Wing. She is regarded as the most openly empowered presidential wife in American history, save for Eleanor Roosevelt.

I recommend getting to know all of these women through reading books about them and/or their writings, and by viewing any television shows or movies that you can find regarding their lives. They are extraordinary women and have helped to shape the lives for all of us women in the twenty-first century.

I respect and applaud all the women in our past and current history who have helped us become the women we are today in the twenty-first century. And I applaud each of *you*. I ask you now to look within. Identify your strengths and improve on them. Identify your weaknesses and work on those. Identify your gifts and use those gifts. In Oprah's words, "Live your best life." Your accomplishments can be greater than you know.

# Chapter Nine

# Embracing Each Other's Differences: All Relationships Are Valuable

*"In Germany they first came for the Communists, and I didn't speak up because I wasn't a Communist. Then they came for the Jews, and I didn't speak up because I wasn't a Jew. Then they came for the trade unionists, and I didn't speak up because I wasn't a trade unionist. Then they came for the Catholics, and I didn't speak up because I was a Protestant. Then they came for me—and by that time no one was left to speak up."*
~Reverend Martin Niemoller

As you may have observed in your reading of the previous chapter (which highlighted some of our prominent women in history), our world is comprised of very diverse individuals—all with many talents, unique characteristics, and different views of the world and the people who live in it. Look around and you will see that our society is very diverse. Diversity enriches our lives and makes them more interesting than we can imagine. Cultural diversity brings together the resources and talents of many people for the shared benefit of all; however, the differences among us are the basis of fear, bigotry, and even violence. By learning to recognize and appreciate our differences, we will find that we are more alike than we are different. We can overcome our fears and intolerance by getting to know people who are different from us. All of us can help create a world that is good for us (by helping one another)—a world that helps us learn and grow from the knowledge gained from one another.

People may fear diversity, simply because they are accustomed to the way things used to be…and many people do not want to adjust to change. Change makes many of us uncomfortable; many people feel uncomfortable because of the unknown. Others may somehow feel threatened because they may lose control or power. They do not take the time or the opportunity to get to know people of a different culture. We know that knowledge is power. That which we do not know can lead to fear and resentment and even bigotry. These fears can often be countered through education.

Our lives are made better when we understand and appreciate individual differences. It has been said that "if you gain a new language, you gain a new world." There is so much that we can teach to and learn from others in a mutually supportive effort to acquire respect for everyone. Lack of respect is often based on ignorance or misinformation. If you do not understand another's values and/or beliefs, then it is much easier to have negative thoughts about him/her. And so we see the seeds of prejudice and intolerance among people sown.

People (in general) have always been prejudiced about things that are different from themselves; people are prejudiced against different people. They probably will always judge others because of race, body image, creed, nationality, socioeconomic status, educational status, and more. Those who do this are missing learning experiences about how can we be the best mothers, daughters, sisters, and friends that we can be. We should look forward to being more open to others and embracing each other's differences.

Well, I can say this with certainty: In your own circle of family and friends, you are different from each and every one of them. You might be similar to some of them, but, most certainly, you are different—and your differences are to be acknowledged and embraced, because you are beautifully and wonderfully made.

It is important that we celebrate *all women* and not just those who are famous or who do great things, as discussed in the last chapter. Let us focus on embracing each other's differences as women—realizing that all of us are valuable, and all relationships are valuable.

---

*"Much of the vitality of a friendship lies in the honoring of differences, not simply in the enjoyment of similarities."*
~Author Unknown

---

Different women make different choices. These choices can be based on talents, ages, races, religions, or marital statuses; therefore, it is obvious that our differences will make us who we are. When acknowledging those differences, use those words to inspire others rather than bring them down. Here are some ideas to help women come together (as stated before), learn from each other, celebrate our diversity, and embrace each other's differences.

### *Look at Yourself (Accept Who You Are)*

As women, the way we treat other women is a reflection of our fears and insecurities about ourselves. Self-acceptance is the first step to embracing the differences—but, we women tend to be haunted by our own self-talk. *Am I too large? Am I too dark? Are my breasts too small (or too large)? Is that a wrinkle? Is that cellulite? Did he notice me? Is she prettier than I am?* And the list goes on and on.

Life is about being the best that we can be. We can spoil male and female relationships by focusing on our insecurities. Relationships need work and that work has to come from you. Think of it this way: You need good soil. You plant a garden; then, you water it and nurture it and help it grow. You love it. You love every plant, treating each with care.

These relationships include your children also. You can care for your children and continue to pursue a career, change your career, or take classes to enhance the career that you already have. Many mothers feel guilty if/when they want to pursue an education or a career. They think, "I have small children. Why do I want to leave them and go out and have a career?" I used to wonder about my own vocation. I continued to attend school while my children were very young. I have had friends who are mothers who felt content and fulfilled without complicating their lives with school or a career. Now, I have a deeper appreciation of my own personal desires and goals, making it easier to embrace other women's choices. I applaud each of you for your choices.

One of my friends once said that one of the main reasons why we feel threatened by other women's choices is due to a feeling of insecurity about our own choices. It is up to all of us to be at peace with the choices that we have made.

### Look "Ahead" (Appreciate What Is Behind You)

Our wanting to be like other women or feeling as though other women "should be more like me" can create feelings of judgment and criticism that will prevent you from having a long-lasting friendship. Look for your positives in yourself and be happy with who you are. Focusing on others can lead to self-criticism, self-judgment, low self-worth, and anxiety.

Recently, there was a discussion about "working moms" versus "stay-at-home moms." Most mothers I know (including myself) work very hard at whatever the task when it involves their children. Women are dedicated to doing the best for their children at all times.

Perhaps we should all start by being honest about the inherent struggles that come with each of these choices. If both "sides" felt comfortable being open about their lives, then it would make everyone feel less defensive and find some common ground.

There is pressure on both sides of the working mom versus stay-at-home-mom issue. We can examine the social aspect, the religious aspect, the pressure we feel from the need to be at home when we are at work, and the financial needs that will be met when we are working outside the home.

We must realize that every woman—as well as every family—is different. We must let go of the pressure and negative thoughts that we feel from others. We need to support and love one another, regardless of our differences. "Focus on what is ahead."

### Look for Differences to "Inspire You" (Learn from Those Differences)

If you find yourself getting caught in the "I want what she has" syndrome, then examine yourself. Look at your insecurities and create what you want. Dream your own dreams. Do not settle for second best. Allow what she has to inspire you to create what you want. You do not have to spend a lifetime following in someone's footsteps and looking for ways to take what they have. You are better than that. If you admire another woman enough to settle for wanting what she has and wanting her life, then she will always be a step ahead of you. Create your own path. Let another woman's gift, skill, or trait be a springboard for the development of that particular gift or character trait *in you*! For example, younger women can look to older women for wisdom from life experiences—and older women can be inspired by younger women's energy, passion, and innovative ways of doing things.

I grew up in a small community and attended a small school (which was not the best school that one could attend), but my mom and dad still expected me and my siblings to be the best that we could be. We did not have a lot of money, but the drive and the motivation for us to always work hard and never give up was an unspoken motto for us children to live by. My mom and dad always expected the best from all of us. They never accepted our failures; they wanted us to be the best at whatever we attempted to do. And because of their love and support, we have all done well. "We are all different."

### Look at Your "Insecurities" (They Help You Move Forward)

Our being critical of others does nothing to enhance who we are. Once we go deeper and get to another's heart and mind, pain and joys, it is so much easier to understand the choices of others and our own choices as well. And once we understand the choices of others, it is easier to celebrate their differences (and ours as well). People start to make sense once we understand their story. It is always good for one to put him-/herself in that other person's shoes. Our choices make sense when we examine our story. It is possible that we will not like what we see, but we must remember that we can change what is to come.

As a school counselor, I found that it was easier to accept and understand someone—even if he/she had made destructive choices—once I knew his/her story. People's stories helped me to understand their motives and reasons for why they did what they did. Their birth orders affected them…and their childhood affected them as well. "Let your insecurities inspire you."

### Look at the Green Grass in "Your Yard" (It Is There)

It is easy to look at the lives of others through jealous and envious eyes when they have what we *think* we want. There are positive aspects to every unpleasant situation. No woman "has it all." Our assessing what others do not have can help us appreciate what it is that we *do* have.

Married women can learn to better appreciate their imperfect relationship from their single friends. Single women can learn to enjoy their independence and freedom by learning of their married friends' relationships. We know that there are positives and negatives to both married life and single life. Talk to those you know. "Listen to everyone's story."

### *Look at the "Unfamiliar" (There Is a Lot to Learn)*

We must get to know people who are different from us; instead of gravitating socially to those who are just like us, we must look for the unfamiliar when we walk into a room. When at a party or gathering of any kind, we should actively seek out someone who is different from us— different age group, different marital status or socioeconomic status, and so forth—while asking ourselves this question: "What can I learn about her? More importantly, what can I learn *from* her?"

We can celebrate the differences with our friends by getting involved in things that they like. We can invite people whom we do not know to participate in fun activities. "Get to know the unfamiliar."

A friend told me that recently, a member of her family was not going to attend a family get-together because there was going to be a family member there who had recently joined a religion that was different from the "family" religion. I was not surprised, but saddened that I was actually hearing this in the twenty-first century. How is this possible? How can people be prejudiced concerning religion in this day and age? It would have never occurred to me to not attend an event because there would be a family member there who now belonged to a different religion. I then realized how lucky I was to be part of a family whose members accept one another (diversities and all). As I thought about it more, I became *thankful—thankful* that I do not live my life like that; *thankful* that we are surrounded by families who are different from us and who embrace these differences. There are all different types of families, cultures, religions, lifestyles, and ideas. And we can learn so much from one another.

### *Look at the "Diversity within Your Family" (We Are All Different)*

When looking at relationships within families, like any relationship there is a dominant person in control of the relationship; however, whether the relationship thrives or withers, it is not up to one person alone to fix it... and one alone does not usually create the conflict. As the saying goes, it takes two to tango. When major family relationship problems are encountered, one family member may try to get the other person to change. Sometimes this approach works, especially if the requests of both the individual and the other person are reasonable—but many times, this strategy just leads to frustration. On the other hand, if a person cannot change another person, then maybe he/she should just accept the other person as he/she is. Another option is for one to change him-/herself in a way that solves the problem. This requires that he/she redefine the problem as an internal one instead of as an external one.

An internal way of one's viewing relationship problems is to consider that they reflect back to him/her a part of him-/herself that he/she dislikes. If a person has a negative external relationship situation, then it is a reflection of a conflict in his/her own thinking. The individual should try looking inside him-/herself and look for ways to change. Once he/she starts looking inside him-/herself for the problem, it may become easier to solve.

But, many times the problem is not that easy to solve. There are times as one problem is being solved that another one surfaces. When there is a problem with a family member, it can be very complicated. What may become obvious in tackling such problems is that an individual may harbor one or more beliefs that perpetuate the relationship problem in its current form. Those beliefs are the real problem—the true cause of the unhealthy relationship.

For example, consider a problematic relationship between yourself and another family member. Suppose you hold the belief that you must be close to every family member simply because he/she is related to you. Perhaps there is a flaw in this person's behavior that you would never accept if it came from a stranger—but since the person is a relative you tolerate it out of a sense of duty, obligation, or simply because he/she is "family." But ask yourself, "Would I tolerate this behavior from a stranger? Then why do I feel that it is all right coming from a family member?" What are the person's beliefs that make it hard for you to continue in the relationship? Are those beliefs really true for you?

Fortunately, my immediate family members work to maintain positive relationships. But that is not the case with all families, and it is not always easy. There is one situation that I am familiar with where several family members have become estranged from one of the other family members. (You probably know families like this, too.) Their differences stem from jealousy, feelings of inadequacy, and being less prosperous than the other family member. This family member has been shut out of the family circle. This, as you can imagine, cannot be a good situation for any of them. This can be corrected with all parties' desire to work at it. Family conflict is painful for everyone involved. Take note when reading the following quote: "We all should know that diversity makes for a rich tapestry, and we must understand that all the threads of the tapestry are equal in value no matter what their color."—Maya Angelou

Despite the differences between members of my family, we are all on good terms with each other and get along well. You cannot always be close friends with everyone in your family; however, you can try and hope that things work out for the best.

Yesterday I was clever, so I wanted to change the world. Today I am wise, so I am changing myself.
—Rumi

If you operate under the assumption that family is forever and that you must remain loyal to all your relatives and you will always be friends, I want you to know that those beliefs are your choices—goals that are not always easy to achieve. If you are fortunate enough to have a close family that is genuinely supportive of the person you are, that is great. You will find the closeness of your family and friends to be a tremendous source of strength. Your loyalty to family closeness will likely be very empowering.

On the other hand, if you find yourself with family relationships that are incompatible with your becoming your best self, then loyalty can cause stress and low self-esteem. Ask yourself whether you are holding yourself back from growing, from achieving your own happiness and fulfillment, and from potentially doing a lot of good for others if family or friends are holding you back.

Loyalty is a worthy quality, but what does it mean for one to be loyal to his/her family or friend? To say the word does not mean that you are practicing loyalty. You are probably familiar with "friends" who utter the word *loyalty*, but will do everything they can to come between friends for self-gain. They will not tell the truth; instead, they will give false information and use it to break up a friendship. Those are the people whom you will probably have to leave behind. After discussing this story with several friends, we concluded that if a person would like to be like you or feels threatened by you and would go to any measure to attain what you have, then friendship with that person is going to be hard to achieve.

---

*"Trying to be like others is hard work, and very difficult to achieve. Achieving love from within and developing that love to embrace who you are is a treasure that no one can take from you."*
~Chris Norris

---

What I am suggesting is that in order to solve family relationship problems, which exist at one level of awareness, you may need to take a look at the other family member and try to understand his/her values and what is important to him/her. It will be helpful for you to take a deeper look at your values, your beliefs, and your definitions of terms like *loyalty* and *family*. Once you resolve those issues, the problems will tend to take care of themselves.

If a relationship is important to you, then it is possible that you will have to find a new way to continue your relationship without conflict— or you will have to accept that you have outgrown the relationship in its current form and then permit yourself to move on to new relationships.

Think of it this way: When you say goodbye to a problematic relationship issue, you are really saying good-bye to an old part of you that you have outgrown. Refuse to hold on to conflict-ridden relationships in your life. When you put negative thoughts out of your mind, you will find yourself putting negative people out of your life.

There is a rainbow at the end of this process of letting go. When you resolve conflicts in your mind, you will attract new relationships that will have a more positive influence on your life.

Change is always good. Many times we attract into our lives more of what we already are. If you do not like the situation you find yourself in, stop thinking the thoughts that attract it. For example, if a family member is too controlling over you, then change the way you react to the situation. When you identify the problem as external, your solutions may take the form of trying to control other people, and you will be met with strong resistance. But when you identify the problem as internal, it is much easier to solve. You may be unable to change a person who exhibits controlling behavior toward you; however, you can change how *you* react to the situation.

When we are identifying and resolving relationship problems, we are forced to look within. And as we become more conscious about our thoughts, our feelings, and how we react to others, our relationships will grow in the way that we hope they will grow. The relationships we have with other people are projections of the relationships we have within ourselves. Our external relationships and our internal relationships are in fact the same relationships. They only seem different because we look at them differently.

An important exercise for you to try is this: Make a list of all the things that bother you about other people. Now reread that list as though it applies to you. Did you find that many of your complaints about others are really complaints about yourself? Take a close look and think about the answer.

Jealousy is a fact of life. There are times when "a friend" wants what the other friend has. I am familiar with a situation where one friend said to another, "I want to be like you." The friend did not know at that time what she would do to achieve that goal. Well, she worked hard to take her friend's boyfriend (even though she was a newlywed). Examine your thoughts from all sides. Take a look at your friends. Then go to work on things that you want to change about yourself and look at what could be preventing you from achieving your goals.

A great way to accelerate your personal growth is to build relationships with others and to extend yourself to those who are different. The more you interact with others, the more you learn about yourself.

Accept yourself, and love yourself as you are. Forgive yourself for problems that you may have caused. Analyze all parts of yourself. Accept and love everyone. Make changes (if that is your choice). The more you improve your internal relationships between your thoughts, beliefs, and intentions, the more loving and harmonious your human relationships will become. Love unconditionally—love in your heart and mind—and you will see it reflected in your reality. And this will be reflected in your relationships as a mother, a daughter, a sister, and a friend.

I think that the most profound thing I can leave with you about your relationships is that they are all valuable. We learn from each other; we grow because of each other. Nurture those people in your life and know that they are there for a reason.

As I leave you, I encourage you to embrace yourself as a powerful and loving woman, mother, daughter, sister, and friend. Be the best you can be and know that *that* is enough.

---

*"Remember, with God's help,*
*there are no failures in life—only learning experiences*
*(some harder than others)."*
~Chris Norris

---

# Resources & Reading Suggestions

*Chicken Soup for the Sister's Soul: Inspirational Stories About Sisters and Their Changing Relationships*
By Jack Canfield, Mark Victor Hansen, Patty Mitchell, Nancy Mitchell, Katy McNamara, Heather McNamara
Publisher: HCI; Early Edition (October 31, 2002)

*My Sister, My Self: Understanding the Sibling Relationship That Shapes Our Lives, Our Loves, and Ourselves*
By Vikki Stark
Publisher: McGraw-Hill; 1 edition (September 5, 2006)

*Mom Loves You Best: Forgiving and Forging Sibling Relationships*
By Cathy Cress, Kali Cress Peterson
Publisher: New Horizon Press (October 1, 2010)

*Why Can't We Get Along: Healing Adult Sibling Relationships*
By Peter Goldenthal
Publisher: Wiley; 1 edition (April 5, 2002)

*Sisters: An Anthology*
By Jan Freeman, Emily Wojcik, Deborah Bull
Publisher: Paris Press (December 1, 2009)

*Just Sisters: You Mess With Her, You Mess With Me*
By Bonnie Louise Kuchler
Publisher: Willow Creek Press (October 2006)

*Sisters: A Force to Be Reckoned With*
By Bonnie Louise Kuchler
Publisher: Willow Creek Books (August 1, 2011)

*When You and Your Mother Can't Be Friends: Resolving the Most Complicated Relationship of Your Life*
By Victoria Secunda
Publisher: Delta (May 1, 1991)

*Letter to My Daughter*
By Maya Angelou
Publisher: Random House Trade Paperbacks; Trade Paperback Edition (October 27, 2009)

*Margaret Sanger: A Life of Passion*
By Jean H. Baker
Publisher: Hill and Wang; First Edition (November 8, 2011)

*Sibling Revelry: 8 Steps to Successful Adult Sibling Relationships*
By Joann Levitt, Marjory Levitt, Joel Levitt
Publisher: Dell Publishing (July 3, 2001)

*I Thought We'd Never Speak Again: The Road from Estrangement to Reconciliation*
By Laura Davis
Publisher: Harper Perennial (April 29, 2003)

*The Sister Knot: Why We Fight, Why We're Jealous, and Why We'll Love Each Other No Matter What*
By Terri Apter
Publisher: W. W. Norton & Company (January 17, 2008)